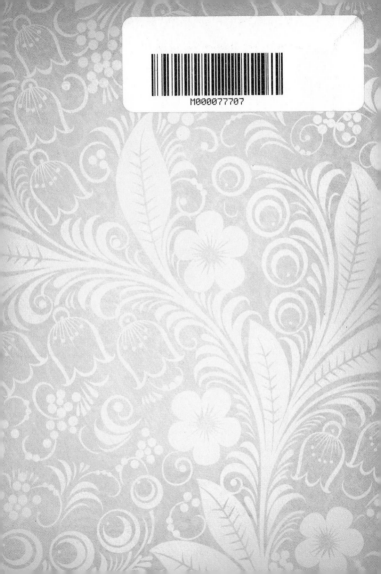

Circle of Friends

Shared Hope

Inspiration for a Woman's Soul

BARBOUR
PUBLISHING

Circle of Friends is a ministry of women helping women. Born out of a small accountability group that led to a women's Bible study, Circle of Friends Ministries is now a nonprofit organization dedicated to encouraging women to find and follow Christ. Our desire is to encourage one another to love God more deeply and to follow Him with a heart of passion that reaches out and draws others along with us on our journey.

"Circle of Friends are women of biblical depth and compassion for others. They have a knack for bringing humor, hope, and practical application to everyday situations."

—Carol Kent, speaker and author
When I Lay My Isaac Down and *A New Kind of Normal*

"Circle of Friends has its finger on the pulse of the heart-needs of women today. Through word and song they link arms with women around the globe to bring the hope and healing of Jesus Christ."

—Sharon Jaynes, speaker and author
Becoming a Woman Who Listens to God and
Extraordinary Moments with God

ISBN 978-1-61626-201-3

Published by Barbour Publishing, Inc., P.O. Box 719, Uhrichsville, Ohio 44683, www.barbourbooks.com

Our mission is to publish and distribute inspirational products offering exceptional value and biblical encouragement to the masses.

Member of the
Evangelical Christian
Publishers Association

Printed in India.

Introduction

Who can understand the heart of a woman—with all its joys and triumphs, challenges and heartaches—better than another woman? We are told in Titus that mature women of the faith are to be "teachers of good things," and in Hebrews that we are to "exhort (encourage) one another daily."

Shared Hope is a devotional written by women who have a passion and love for Jesus. Their stories, insights, biblical applications, and refreshing honesty in everyday trials in their lives will encourage your heart and strengthen your faith. So grab a cup of coffee or tea, pull up a chair, and share life, share hope, with your "Circle of Friends." You'll laugh, you'll cry, you'll find that you have truly found a place to belong. . . .

Hope in Suffering

"But I have this against you,
that you have left your first love."

REVELATION 2:4 NASB

One of my favorite questions to ask couples over dinner is "How did you meet?" Each story invariably presents a set of impossible circumstances that had to be orchestrated in order to bring this man and woman together. As these details are relayed, a glow begins to come back into the eyes of those remembering. There is nothing to compare with that "first bloom of love."

This is the kind of love which God desires from us. That on-fire, totally consuming, single focus of our attention. His call to the church at Ephesus then was that they remember their first love—and rekindle their purpose to seek Him first.

His message, however, to the church at Smyrna was very different. "'I know your tribulation and your poverty (but you are rich). . . . Do not fear what you are about to suffer. . . . Be faithful until death, and I will give you the crown of life'" (Revelation 2:9–10 NASB).

Throughout history, God's church has suffered persecution. But here is a message of hope to all for whom cruelty is a constant companion: "Remain faithful, God's reward is at hand."

CAROL L. FITZPATRICK
Daily Wisdom for Women

Divine Appointments

Jesus said, "Take care of my sheep."
JOHN 21:16 NIV

A beautiful young woman stumbled into the airplane obviously exhausted. She was dressed in skintight jeans, a distracting, low-cut T-shirt, and sunglasses that hid something. . .but I wasn't sure what.

"They messed up my ticket, and I don't have a seat," she complained to the flight attendant.

"This one's empty," I offered, pointing to the seat next to me.

I pulled out my book, *Your Scars Are Beautiful to God*, to prepare for an upcoming interview, but I sensed God saying, *Put down the book and talk to this girl.*

God, she doesn't want to talk, I argued.

Put down the book and talk to this girl.

I put down my book and turned to my fellow passenger.

"Where are you headed?" I asked.

"Home."

"Where's home?"

"A small town I'm sure you've never heard of." Then she glanced down at the book in my lap.

"Scars. Well, I've certainly got a lot of those."

"So do I," I said. "That's why I wrote the book."

"You wrote it?" She was surprised.

For the next hour and a half, this young girl poured out her heart to me. She had been abandoned, sexually abused, and misused. As I prayed for her, tears spilled down her cheeks to wash away the years of regret.

We parted ways, but the memory lingered. God allowed me to apply His healing salve to the wounds of one of His little lambs.

There was no mix-up in her airline ticket; she had a divine seat assignment made by God.

SHARON JAYNES
Extraordinary Moments with God

A New Song

Sing a new song to the LORD, for he has done wonderful deeds. His right hand has won a mighty victory; his holy arm has shown his saving power!

PSALM 98:1 NLT

Who needs a new song? Do you ever get tired of the old tune? I do! A new song! Spiritually, many of us need a new song to sing. Some of us are sung out, tired of singing solo or of being lost in a big choir where no one notices our contribution! God can give us a new song to sing. It will start when we meet with God and tune in to the vibrations of heaven. Songs you've never sung before have a fresh, sweet, winsome sound that alerts those around you to the state of your soul. God gave me a new song when my children got married, when my husband had to be away a lot, and when I got sick and had to have a scary operation. They were new songs because I'd never been in those situations, and new situations require new songs. They were not always happy songs, but who says all songs are happy ones? A minor key can be just as pretty as a major one.

The important thing is to sing a song—a new song of faith and hope, of self-discovery or God-discovery, at every turn of the road, every station, every resting place. Just today I asked Him to help me find something to sing about as I washed up a pile of dirty dishes. He helped me to compose a new song over the kitchen sink. God is never stuck for a tune. New songs are the Spirit's business—ask Him to give you one.

JILL BRISCOE
The One Year Book of Devotions for Women

Hope of Better Things

*Still another said, "I will follow you, Lord; but first
let me go back and say good-by to my family."
Jesus replied, "No one who puts his hand to the plow
and looks back is fit for service in the kingdom of God."*

LUKE 9:61–62 NIV

Jesus had "resolutely set out for Jerusalem" (verse
51) but several of His followers failed to count
the cost of discipleship. Jesus knew this man who
wanted to first "go back" to his family had a longing
for his old life. No one can move in two directions
at once. It is impossible to go forward when you
are looking to the past. A man who plows a field
looking over his shoulder plows a crooked furrow,
which means disaster for the whole field.

Jesus calls us to set our minds, our wills, and
our hearts to follow Him. If we live with a divided
mind or heart, longing for the things of this world,
we will end up like the rich man in Luke 18:22 who

"went away sorrowful." He loved his life of wealth more than he loved the Lord and could not commit to following Him.

To be fit for His service, to join the fellowship of His followers, we must first let go of anything we hold in more esteem than our Savior. When our fists are tightly clutched around our own plans and longings, we lose out on what God wants to give us. We need to open our hand, release everything, and allow God to fill our lives with something better— His plan for us.

Missy Horsfall
Circle of Friends

The King's Prosperity

A King shall reign and prosper.

JEREMIAH 23:5 KJV

*I*f we are really interested, heart and soul, in a person, how delighted we are to have positive assurance of his prosperity, and how extremely interested and pleased we feel at hearing anything about it! Is not this a test of our love to our King? Are we both interested and happy in the short, grand, positive words which are given us about His certain prosperity? If so, the pulse of our gladness is beating true to the very heart of God.

If we could get one glimpse of our King in His present glory and joy, how we who love Him would rejoice for Him and with Him! And if we could get one great view of the wide but hidden prosperity of His kingdom at this moment, where would be our discouragement and faint-heartedness! Many

Christians nowadays are foregoing an immense amount of cheer, because they do not take the trouble to inquire, or read, or go where they can hear about the present prosperity of His kingdom. Those who do not care much can hardly be loving much or helping much.

But we do care about it; and so how jubilantly the promises of His increasing prosperity ring out to us!

FRANCES RIDLEY HAVERGAL
Daily Thoughts for the King's Children

I Think I Can

*I can do everything through
him who gives me strength.*

PHILIPPIANS 4:13 NIV

Remember the Little Golden Book about the little engine that could? You know the story. He tries really hard—against many odds—chugging along and puffing, "I think I can, I think I can" until he proves everyone wrong and reaches his goal. I've always loved that little book. You know why? Because it's packed with powerful teaching. If we can keep a can-do attitude, we can achieve many things.

My eleven-year-old daughter, Abby, is a great gymnast. In fact, she is a member of a competitive gymnastics team. When Abby is preparing for her tumbling pass, I can always tell if she's going to do well just by the look on her face. If she approaches the mat with a can-do facial expression, I know she's going to nail it. But if she shows fear on her face, I know she's not going to give her best performance. It's all in the attitude.

Maybe you have a goal that seems impossible to reach—sort of like the little engine that could. Well, God says that you can do all things through Him, so go for it! Keep a can-do attitude, and watch your dreams become a reality!

MICHELLE MEDLOCK ADAMS
Daily Wisdom for Working Women

The Nature of Comfort

My comfort in my suffering is this:
Your promise preserves my life.

PSALM 119:50 NIV

Comfort, whether human or divine, is pure and simple comfort and is nothing else. We none of us care for pious phrases. We want realities; and the reality of being comforted and comfortable seems to me almost more delightful than any other thing in life. We all know what it is. When as little children we have cuddled up into our mother's lap after a fall or a misfortune, and have felt her dear arms around us, and her soft kisses on our hair, we have had comfort. When as grown-up people after a hard day's work we have put on our slippers and seated ourselves by the fire, in an easy chair with a book, we have had comfort. When after a painful illness we have begun to recover and have been able to stretch our limbs and open our eyes without pain, we have had comfort. When someone whom we dearly love has been ill almost unto death and has been restored to us in health again, we have had comfort. A thousand times in our lives probably have we said, with a sigh of relief, as of toil over or burdens laid off, "Well this is comfortable," and in that word *comfortable* there has been comprised more of rest, and relief, and satisfaction, and pleasure, than any other word glory of the religion of the Lord Jesus Christ.

He was anointed to comfort "all that mourn." The "God of all comfort" sent His Son to be the comforter of a mourning world. And all through His life on earth He fulfilled His divine mission. The God of all Comfort enfolds life's trials and pains in an all-embracing peace.

HANNAH WHITALL SMITH
The God of All Comfort

A Grand Promise

Uphold me according to your promise, that I may live,
and let me not be put to shame in my hope.

PSALM 119:116 NRSV

Perhaps there is no point in which expectation has been so limited by experience as this. We believe God is able to do for us just so much as He has already done, and no more. We take it for granted a line must be drawn somewhere; and so we choose to draw it where experience ends, and faith would have to begin. Even if we have trusted and proved Him as to keeping our members and our minds, faith fails when we would go deeper and say, "Keep my will!" And the result of this, as of every other faithless conclusion, is either discouragement and depression, or, still worse, acquiescence in an unyielded will, as something that can't be helped.

Now let us turn from our thoughts to God's thoughts. Verily, they are not as ours! He says He is able to do exceedingly abundantly above all that we ask or think. Apply this here.

We ask Him to take our wills and make them His. Does He or does He not mean what He says? And if He does, should we not trust Him to do this thing that we have asked and longed for, and not less, but more? Is anything too hard for the Lord? Hath He said, and shall He not do it? Does He mock our longing by acting as I have seen an older person act to a child, by accepting some trifling gift of no intrinsic value, just to please the little one, and then throwing it away as soon as the child's attention is diverted? We give Him no opportunity (so to speak) of proving His faithfulness to this great promise, but we will not fulfill the condition of reception, believing it.

It is most comforting to remember that the grand promise, "Thy people shall be willing in the day of Thy power," is made by the Father to Christ Himself. The Lord Jesus holds this promise, and God will fulfill it to Him. He will make us willing because He has promised Jesus He will do so.

FRANCES RIDLEY HAVERGAL
Kept for the Master's Use

Hope in Purpose

"For I know the plans I have for you," declares the
LORD, *"plans to prosper you and not to harm you,*
plans to give you hope and a future."

We all need to have a sense of why we are here.
We all need to know we were created for a purpose.
We will never find fulfillment and happiness until
we are doing the thing for which we were created.
But God won't move us into the big things He has
called us to unless we have been proven faithful in
the small things He has given us. So if you are doing what you deem to be small things right now, rejoice! God's getting you ready for big things ahead.

Don't think for a moment that if you haven't
moved into the purposes God has for you by now
that it's too late. It is *never* too late. I did everything

late. I didn't come to the Lord until I was twenty-eight. I got married late, had children late, and I didn't even start writing professionally until I was over forty. My whole ministry happened when I was in my forties and most of it in my fifties. Trust me, if you are still breathing, God has a purpose for you. He has something for you to do *now*.

STORMIE OMARTIAN
The Power of a Praying Woman

Rich Promises

I will bless you [with abundant increase of favors]. . .
and you will be a blessing [dispensing good to others].
GENESIS 12:2 AMP

The Bible is full of God's blessings for our lives, full of positive words, promises granted to those who choose to follow Him, who choose to believe in His assurances. Hebrews 11:8 tells us that "by faith Abraham obeyed when he was called to go out to the place which he would receive as an inheritance" and that "he went out, not knowing where he was going" (NKJV). And when Abraham arrived at his destination, God *met him there* and gave him a brand-new promise: "I will bless you. . . and you will be a blessing" (Genesis 12:2 AMP). As sons and daughters of Abraham (see Galatians 3:7), we share in this promise! We can be filled with assurance that wherever we go, God will bless us. He is even going before us, ready to greet us with a word of encouragement when we get there.

Is your faith strong enough and your mind open enough to make room for God's bounty of blessings? Or is your faith too little, your mind too closed? Perhaps you feel you are undeserving. If so, plant the words of Hebrews 11:6 in your heart: "Without faith it is impossible to please and be satisfactory to Him. For whoever would come near to God must [necessarily] believe that God exists and that He is the rewarder of those who earnestly and diligently seek Him [out]" (AMP). Claim the promise of 1 John 5:14–15: "Now this is the confidence that we have in Him, that if we ask anything according to His will, He hears us. And if we know that He hears us, whatever we ask, we know that we have the petitions that we have asked of Him" (NKJV). It's not a matter of deserving but of firm faith, great expectation, and sincere seeking.

DONNA K. MALTESE
Power Prayers to Start Your Day

Hope in Song

"Hear, O kings; give ear, O rulers!
I—to the LORD, I will sing, I will sing
praise to the LORD, the God of Israel."

JUDGES 5:3 NASB

*I*f you only knew, dear hesitating friends, what strength and gladness the Master gives when we loyally sing forth the honor of His name, you would not forego it! Oh, if you only knew the difficulties it saves! For when you sing "always and only for your King," you will not get much entangled by the King's enemies. Singing an out-and-out sacred song often clears one's path at a stroke as to many other things. If you only knew the rewards He gives, very often then and there, the recognition that you are one of the King's friends by some lonely and timid one; the openings which you quite naturally gain of speaking a word for Jesus to hearts which, without the song, would never have given you the chance! If you only knew the joy of believing that His sure promise, "My Word

28

shall not return unto Me void" will be fulfilled as you *sing* that word for Him! If you only tasted the solemn happiness of knowing that you have indeed a royal audience, that the King Himself is listening as you sing! If you only knew and why should you not know? Shall not the time past of your life suffice you for the miserable, double-hearted, calculating service? Let Him have the *whole* use of your voice at any cost, and see if He does not put many a totally unexpected new song into your mouth!

I am not writing all this to great and finished singers, but to everybody who can sing at all. Those who think they have only a very small talent, are often most tempted not to trade with it for their Lord. Whether you have much or little natural voice, there is reason for its cultivation and room for its use. Place it at your Lord's disposal, and He will show you how to make the most of it for Him; for not seldom His multiplying power is brought to bear on a consecrated voice.

FRANCES RIDLEY HAVERGAL
Kept for the Master's Use

Jesus Is Coming!

"Therefore you also be ready, for the Son of Man is coming at an hour you do not expect."

MATTHEW 24:44 NKJV

Look at it from the non-Christian point of view: We Christians say the person we love most in all time and eternity will return to us, bypassing death and the grave and coming again in glory. This person isn't a sweetheart, spouse, or much-loved parent. As much as we're devoted to the folks we share earth with, we claim they cannot give us hope because they cannot conquer death.

This hope in Jesus seems silly to the world. Though we've never met Him face-to-face, we believe He still lives. Our hearts belong entirely to this unseen One. Without viewing Him in the flesh, we believe He will return. How can anyone understand such attitudes unless they, too, have met the Savior?

We tell them that the One we trust in said He's coming again. Do we completely rely on that seemingly impossible fact? Do we know He could come at any hour, any day? And are we ready for Him to appear? If we're ready, we're living every day as if we could see His face for the first time. Is this the unexpected hour?

PAMELA MCQUADE
Daily Wisdom for the Workplace

Vision of Hope

*Be stunned and amazed, blind yourselves
and be sightless; be drunk, but not from
wine, stagger, but not from beer.*

ISAIAH 29:9 NIV

It has always been my favorite theory that the blind can accomplish nearly everything that may be done by those who can see. Do not think that those who are deprived of physical vision are shut out from the best that earth has to offer her children. There are a few exceptions that instantly come to my mind. For example, through the medium of sight alone, does the astronomer mark the courses, the magnitudes and the varied motions of all the heavenly bodies; and only through the medium of the eye can the sculptor produce a beautiful statue from the rude and uncut marble. So, likewise, of the painter.

From attaining high rank in these fine arts the blind of necessity, are debarred; but not so from poetry and music, in which the mind gives us a true image of the reality. Almost every lad at school is able to relate stray bits of legendary lore of ancient and modern artists who have been blind. Indeed, who can forget Euclid, the blind geometrician; or Homer, the blind bard; or Milton, the author?

A great many people fancy that the blind learn music only by ear, never by note; and yet a number of musical experts have told me that their blind pupils learn as proficiently as others by the latter method. It is truly wonderful—marvelous—to what a degree the memory can be trained, not only by those who rely upon it for most of their knowledge of the external world, but by all who wish to add to their general intellectual culture. But why should the blind be regarded as objects of pity? Darkness may indeed throw a shadow over the outer vision; but there is no cloud, however dark, that can keep the sunlight of hope from the trustful soul.

FANNY CROSBY
Memories of Eighty Years

Water of Life

Come near to God and he will come near to you.

JAMES 4:8 NIV

O My daughter, shall I speak unto thee as one whose voice is lost in the noise of crashing surf, or as one who calls in vain in the midst of a deep forest, where there is no ear to hear nor voice to respond? Will ye be as an instrument with broken strings from which the musician can bring forth no music?

Nay, I would have you to be as the waterfall whose sound is continuous, and as a great river whose flow is not interrupted. Ye shall not sing for a time and then be silent for a season. Ye shall not praise for a day, and then revert to the current topics of everyday life.

Ye shall never exhaust My supply. The more ye give, the more will be given unto thee. Ye are in a learning process. I have much to share with thee; yea, out of the abundance of My heart would I instruct thee. I would teach you truths of heavenly wisdom which ye cannot learn from the lips of man. I will instruct thee in the way that thou shalt go. From whom else can ye inquire?

I will bring My love and My life to thee. From whence have ye any such comfort and strength elsewhere? The more often ye come to Me to draw of this water of Life, the more shall thy life be enriched in wisdom—yes, but also in many other ways. Ye have need of My grace that ye may share My truth with a right spirit. Ye need to keep thy channel straight and clear, that My blessing be not hindered in flowing through thee, and that the waters may be kept pure.

FRANCES J. ROBERTS
Come Away My Beloved

Getting Zinged

"Bless those who curse you,
pray for those who mistreat you."

LUKE 6:28 NIV

*L*et's be honest; we've all been zinged. You know, those comments that are said so sweetly that it isn't until you walk away that you realize you were insulted, like, "I *love* your hair; it looks like something from the forties." Yeah, I loved hearing that one.

As an individual who is blessed to breathe air, you're sure to have received a zinger. And as women, we've been blessed with long memories that allow us to relive those comments over and over again.

When the zingers come—and they *will* come—you have two choices. You can respond emotionally, leaving godly grace at the door, or you can respond in love—either by remaining silent or by *gently* responding to the comment. The choice is yours.

However, if you're listening to the Holy Spirit, you know that He won't let you get away with responding with a verbal assault. No, it's much better to respond in love. And the next time you see the "zingee," follow the advice found in Luke 6:28, and pray for God's blessing in her life. As you do, God promises that "your reward will be great" (Luke 6:35), and you will become more and more like Him.

GENA MASELLI
Daily Wisdom for Working Women

Our New Name

*You will be called by a new name that
the mouth of the LORD will bestow.*

ISAIAH 62:2 NIV

The God of the Universe loves us passionately. In spite of this, we have thought of ourselves based on how we feel or others' expectations of us. But there is a truth that changes lives, transforms hearts and minds. It is a truth that sets us free from chains that have restrained us for years. We have been given a new identity, a true identity—an identity that Christ died to give us.

Regardless of past sins or ongoing struggles, God is taken with us. The Bible says that He has loved us with an everlasting love and cheers us along with His loving-kindness. He has clothed us with garments of salvation and arrayed us in robes of righteousness like a bride who adorns herself with jewels. As a groom rejoices over his bride, so God rejoices over us and declares us as lovely.

While on the cross, Jesus Christ took our sin and gave us His righteousness.

We have an identity in Him that cannot be stripped away by anyone or anything. We still make mistakes. But as we go to Him with repentant hearts, He forgives and cleanses us, and calls us restored.

We have been given names that we were never meant to answer to. We have named ourselves out of our own yearning to find a place to belong. But the good news is, Jesus has come to give us a new name. And it's time we start answering to it.

JOCELYN HAMSHER
Circle of Friends

The Lovely Will of God

Let God transform you into a new person by changing the way you think. Then you will learn to know God's will for you, which is good and pleasing and perfect.

ROMANS 12:2 NLT

Formerly it had seemed to me that His will was the terrible instrument of His severity and that I must do all I could to avert its terrors from swooping down upon my devoted head. Now I saw that it was impossible for the will of unselfish love to be anything but good and kind.

It was not that life was to have no more trials, for this wise and loving will might see that trials were a necessary gift of love. Neither was it essential that we should be able to *see* the Divine hand in every trial. Because He loves us with an unselfish and limitless love, He cannot fail to make the apparently hard or cruel or even wicked thing work together for our best good.

No matter who starts our trial, if God permits it to reach us, He has made the trial His own and will turn it for us into a chariot of love which will carry our souls to a place of blessing that we could not have reached in any other way.

God's will is the most lovely thing the universe contains for us, not because it always looks or seems the best, but because it cannot help being the best, since it is the will of infinite unselfishness and of infinite love.

HANNAH WHITALL SMITH
The Unselfishness of God

God's Precious Riches

*God will supply all your needs according
to His riches in glory in Christ Jesus.*

PHILIPPIANS 4:19 NASB

When the Bible writers describe our riches in
Jesus Christ, they often use words starting with
"un": joy unspeakable (see 1 Peter 1:8), unsearch-
able riches (see Ephesians 3:8), and unspeakable
gifts (see 2 Corinthians 9:15). It seems as if they
cannot find words to show the abundance the Lord
gives us.

I think the reason is that the boundless
resources of God's promises are celestial. They are
earthly reproductions of heavenly riches in Jesus
Christ, and they are ours under every circumstance.

All of His riches are for us—not to admire,
but to take and keep. The antichrist is marching on
and organizing his army over the whole world, but

we stand on the Lord's side and may accept all His promises.

Too often we are like people who stand in front of the show window of a jewelry store. We admire the beautiful watches, rings, and bracelets, but we do not go in and pay the price in order to possess them. We just walk away! It is through Jesus that God's greatest and most precious promises have become available to us.

CORRIE TEN BOOM
The End Battle

Hope in God's Keeping

You will be secure, because there is hope;
you will look about you and take your rest in safety.

JOB 11:18 NIV

What is to be for Him? We talk sometimes as if, whatever else could be subdued unto Him, self could never be. But our true self is the new self, taken and won by the love of God, and kept by the power of God.

And kept *for Him!* Why should it be thought a thing incredible with you, when it is only the fulfilling of His own eternal purpose in creating us? "This people have 1 formed *for Myself.*" Not ultimately only, but presently and continually; for he says, "Thou shalt abide *for Me,*" and, "He that remaineth, even he shall *before our God.*" Are you one of His people by faith in Jesus Christ? Then see what you are to Him. You, personally and individually, are part of the Lord's portion (Deuteronomy 32: 9) and of His inheritance (1 Kings 8: 53, and Ephesians 1:18). His portion and inheritance would not be complete without you. You are His peculiar treasure (Exodus 19:5); a *special* people (how warm, and loving, and natural that expression is!), *'unto Himself'* (Deuteronomy 7:6). Would you call it "keeping," if you had a special treasure, a darling little child, for instance, and let it run wild into all sorts of dangers all day long,—sometimes at your side, and sometimes out in the street, with only the intention of fetching it safe home at night? If ye then, being evil, would know better and do better than that, how much more shall our Lord's keeping be true, and tender, and continual, and effectual, when He declares us to be His peculiar treasure, purchased (see 1 Peter 2: 9) for Himself at such unknown cost!

FRANCES RIDLEY HAVERGAL
Kept for the Master's Use

Focus and Balance

But more than anything else, put
God's work first and do what he wants.
Then the other things will be yours as well.

MATTHEW 6:33 CEV

$\mathscr{I}$ constantly struggle with my priorities. I think
they are all in order, and then I find that in a very
short time, I have to work on them again. Plus I
am sure that I have attention deficit disorder. These
disorders were not discovered when I was young,
but I start five major projects all at one time, and
my mind goes in ten directions at once, jumping
from one thing to another so quickly that I can't
even keep up. Consequently, I tend to become too
busy very quickly.

Being too busy is enemy number one to my to-
do list. I get talked into so many good things. One

of the most difficult things for me is to say no to something or someone. Yet when I look at my list, whether mental or written, and examine it before the Lord, I often have to say no in order to be obedient to Him. He has given each of us the ability and freedom to say no; we just don't use it.

Thomas á Kempis reminds us that, just as it is often our duty to do what we don't particularly want to do, it is also our duty at times to leave undone what we want to do. Making and keeping our priorities in order and balanced takes a conscious effort and involves making conscious decisions.

GIGI GRAHAM TCHIVIDJIAN
A Quiet Knowing

A Courageous Queen

For momentary, light affliction is producing for us an eternal weight of glory far beyond all comparison.

2 CORINTHIANS 4:17 NASB

Katie was only eleven years old when the doctors removed her cancerous leg below the knee. She felt her young life was over.

"Who will ever want me?" she cried. "I'll never be able to walk or run again."

Katie did learn how to walk, and life returned to a new kind of normal, though she kept her prosthesis hidden from the world. But then God began nudging Katie to return to the hospital where she had her surgery to talk to other children facing similar ordeals. She put her fears aside and visited the cancer ward and showed a girl named Amanda her leg.

"Here, go ahead and touch it," she said. "It's okay." And Katie saw something flicker in Amanda's eyes. It was hope. . . .

Katie decided it was time to stop hiding her leg from the world, and she did it in a big way. She entered the Miss University of Central Arkansas pageant! She participated in the talent, evening gown, and interview competitions. But she won the heart of the crowd when she proudly walked down the catwalk during the bathing suit competition. . . . I daresay there was never a more precious moment than when Katie Signaigo was crowned Miss UCA.

No, Katie's life was not over when the doctors removed her leg to save her. It was the beginning of an exciting journey filled with many extraordinary moments with God.

SHARON JAYNES
Extraordinary Moments with God

Knowing God Brings Hope

Shout for joy to the LORD, all the earth. Worship the
LORD with gladness; come before him with joyful songs.
Know that the LORD is God. It is he who made us, and
we are his; we are his people, the sheep of his pasture.

PSALM 100:1–3 NIV

In the middle of this psalm of thanksgiving comes
this little nugget of spiritual gold, "Know that the
LORD is God." It may seem random, but when we
look closer we find it isn't out of place at all.

When we know who God is, it lays a founda-
tion upon which we can build our lives. We can
shout and sing in His presence because we know
who we are praising and why. Our worship has a
focus, an object of adoration—a holy and righteous
God. He is the One who made us and we belong
to Him. That is where our thanksgiving and praise
come from!

He is good. He pours out mercy and grace in

an unending stream. His truth endures generation after generation. Knowing all these things—who God is, what He has done, and that He has chosen us and will take care of us—gives us a bedrock of faith to stand upon when circumstances overwhelm us. We are not shaken, we are not moved—because we *know*.

MISSY HORSFALL
Circle of Friends

Always a Bright Side

"I will forget my complaint, I will change my expression, and smile."

JOB 9:27 NIV

There is a real art in smiling. Some people smile, or grin, all the time, and it becomes monotonous to those who look at them. These grinning people never seem to think who or what their smile is for. It is as if their mouths were made in that form. Other people have the kind of smile upon their faces that suggests sarcasm. But there are still others, and I have met [women] who had mastered the art, whose smiles are tear chasers. There is something so understanding in their glance and smile that they make you feel that they care for you and want you to be happy. Sometimes when I have been discouraged or depressed by trials all my own, a bright, hopeful smile from someone has cheered me amazingly. In fact, we are very much dependent upon each other for courage and happiness. Then let us be dispensers of joy as we go through life, smiling and glad. If I am in trouble, having acted foolishly in something or other, then I do not appreciate the grinning smile. I would rather the face that looked into mine would express a little understanding and feeling for my trouble or that it would not notice my foolishness at all; when I find a friend who can meet me this way, then that friend becomes a real comfort and joy to me.

Smiles and gladness are like sweet peas in that the more you gather and give away, the more you have. Leave your sweet peas on the vines, and the flowers are soon gone, but gather them closely each day, and they will blossom the more and last the summer through. So save your smiles for special occasions, when there are joys abroad, and you will pretty nearly run out of them altogether, but give them out at every opportunity, and the joy vines of your heart will thrive and grow. Live in the sunshine. Look on the bright side, for always there is a bright side.

MABEL HALE
Beautiful Girlhood

Hope in Surrender

I appeal to you therefore, brothers, by the mercies of God, to present your bodies as a living sacrifice, holy and acceptable to God, which is your spiritual worship.

ROMANS 12:1 ESV

There is no other way for you but to surrender utterly and to cast all your care on the Lord, and leave it there. You must not think of it or brood over it, but must dismiss it from your mind altogether, except whatever degree is necessary for proper self-care. But if your worst fears are confirmed, then you must bow your neck to the yoke and must accept your life as the very best thing that could have come to you.

You can only conquer your trial by submitting to it. But if you will submit, it will become your joy and crown of rejoicing. Lay yourself as a living sacrifice upon God's altar. Say "Yes" to Him about it all. "Yes, Lord, Yes. Your will, not mine. Your good and perfect will! I am content to suffer; I am content to be laid aside, if it is Your sweet will."

I'm sure that you must not always be looking ahead. I am sure you must live just one day at a time, taking no thought of any kind for tomorrow. It is a glorious chance for you to abandon yourself unreservedly to the love and will of your Lord. And I believe if you will do this, it will be the doorway for you into a far deeper relationship with the Lord than you have ever known yet.

HANNAH WHITALL SMITH
The Christian's Secret of a Holy Life

Moses Is in Glory

And behold, two men were talking with Him;
and they were Moses and Elijah, who, appearing
in glory, were speaking of His departure which
He was about to accomplish at Jerusalem.

LUKE 9:30–31 NASB

*I*n case you've been feeling sorry for Moses who
never got to enter the Promised Land, just look at
what God had in store for him. These verses tell us
that Moses and Elijah appeared in glory. But what
does that really mean?

We are not now what we will become. For
whether we die or are taken up by what is referred
to as the Rapture, the Lord will someday allow
this "earthsuit" of ours to fall away and issue us our
"eternity suit."

"For if we believe that Jesus died and rose
again, even so God will bring with Him those who
have fallen asleep in Jesus. . . . For the Lord Himself

will descend from heaven with a shout, with the voice of the archangel, and with the trumpet of God, and the dead in Christ will rise first. Then we who are alive and remain will be caught up together with them in the clouds to meet the Lord in the air, and so we shall always be with the Lord" (1 Thessalonians 4:14, 16–17 NASB).

That day on top of the mountain, at Jesus' Transfiguration, the apostles witnessed Christ's glory and saw Moses and Elijah. And God spoke from the cloud which encompassed them saying, "'This is my Son, whom I have chosen; listen to him'" (Luke 9:35 NIV).

In spite of your life, are you assured of your salvation?

CAROL L. FITZPATRICK
Daily Wisdom for Women

Hope in His Plan

*"Write down the revelation and make it plain on
tablets so that a herald may run with it. For the
revelation awaits an appointed time; it speaks of the
end and will not prove false. Though it linger, wait
for it; it will certainly come and will not delay."*

HABAKKUK 2:2–3 NIV

Deborah is one of my heroes. At a time when
the nation of Israel had strayed far from the worship of Jehovah and had been taken into captivity
by the Canaanites, God raised up Deborah as a
prophet and judge over the nation. Over the period
of her rule, the Israelites gained their freedom as
this courageous woman made wise decisions and
led them into battle. What was the result? The
entire land had peace for forty years. Deborah
fulfilled her destiny because she followed God with
faith and confidence.

We are all needed to make a holy difference

in this world. In fact, God has chosen us to do just that (see John 15:16). God asks you and me to be outrageously convinced that the purpose of our time here on earth is truly significant. . .so convinced that we will not give up the pursuit of the spiritual dreams He has placed in our hearts.

If God is giving you a dream for your life, write the vision down. Describe it. You'll never do what you cannot visualize. Then let God calculate the route and the timing. When He says to move, step out by faith and continue until you reach your destination. He will fulfill the plans He has for you! Trust Him.

JOYCE STRONG
Author, Speaker

Transforming Trust

*Those who know your name will trust in you, for you,
LORD, have never forsaken those who seek you.*

PSALM 9:10 NIV

As we look at the life of Christ and listen to
His words, we can hear God saying, "I am rest for
the weary; I am peace for the storm-tossed; I am
strength for the strengthless; I am wisdom for the
foolish; I am righteousness for the sinful; I am
all that the neediest soul on earth can want; I am
exceeding abundantly, beyond all you can ask or
think, of blessing, and help, and care."

It is a piece of magnificent good news declared
to you in the Bible; and you only need do with it
exactly what you do when any earthly good news is
told you by a reliable earthly source. If the speaker
is trustworthy, you believe what he says, and act
in accordance. And you must do the same here.
If Christ is trustworthy when He tells you that
He is the manifestation of God, you must believe
what He says, and act accordingly. You must take
your stand on His trustworthiness. You must say
to yourself, and to your friends if need be, "I am

going to believe what Christ says about God. No matter what the seemings may be, nor what my own thoughts and feelings are, nor what anybody else may say, I know that what Christ says about God must be true, for He knew, and nobody else does, and I am going to believe Him right straight through, come what may. He says that He was one with God, so all that He was God is, and I will never be frightened of God any more. I will never again let myself think of Him as a stern Lawgiver who is angry with me because of my sins, nor as a hard Taskmaster who demands from me impossible tasks, nor as a far-off unapproachable Deity, who is wrapped up in His own glory, and is indifferent to my sorrows and my fears. All such ideas of God have become impossible, now that I know that Christ was the true manifestation of God."

If we will take our stand on this one fact, that Christ and God are one, with an intelligent comprehension of what it involves, and will refuse definitely and unwaveringly to cherish any thought of God that is at variance with what Christ has revealed, life will be transformed, for us.

HANNAH WHITALL SMITH
The God of All Comfort

Beauty Instead of Ashes

. . .to bestow on them a crown of beauty instead of ashes, the oil of gladness instead of mourning, and a garment of praise instead of a spirit of despair. They will be called oaks of righteousness, a planting of the Lord for the display of his splendor.

ISAIAH 61:3 NIV

God is able to give comfort just when we need it. The past couple of days have been extremely difficult for me because it is the anniversary of the death of my seventeen-year-old daughter.

The beautiful part of the entire situation is that Liz is already in her eternity. She is walking those streets of gold, in total awe of our God! The comforting part is the total and complete miracle that God gave to us—His continual presence and grace in our lives. He has truly turned our mourning to gladness.

The tears shed have served to cleanse our hearts, and allowed us to relieve the sorrow we felt. The best thing that there is about those tears is that God holds all of our tears in a bottle (Psalm 56:8). A few weeks ago, I began praying about these days and was reminded of that scripture about God saving my tears. I asked the Lord just what His plans are for all of the tears that He holds for all of His people. God spoke to my heart and reminded me of yet another scripture, where Jesus performed His first miracle. He turned the water into wine at the wedding at Cana (John 2:1–11).

I wonder. . .

BECKI REISER
Circle of Friends

Hope in His Presence

Then Jesus went to work on his disciples. "Anyone who intends to come with me has to let me lead. You're not in the driver's seat; I am. Don't run from suffering; embrace it. Follow me and I'll show you how."

MATTHEW 16:24 MSG

My little one, come close to Me. I have consolations for your soul that surpass your sharpest grief. I have walked through the deepest waters, and I am with you as you experience your baptism of sorrow. It is the path that leads to the gate of glory, and the Father waits to greet you there. It is not heaven of which I speak. It is a blessedness of spirit which is given to those who have passed through tribulations, have washed their robes, and have set their feet on the highroad of absolute surrender. From this place there is no turning back. Having passed this point, there is no way to retreat.

Nothing whatever that may be demanded daunts the totally committed. It is the Father's good pleasure to give you the kingdom. Boundless is His love, and with great tenderness, He woos you into a place of favoritism. It may cost you all, but you cannot fathom what He has in store for you.

Hold fast to His hand. He will not lead anywhere except He be present all the time and all the way. Blessed fellowship and holy comfort!

FRANCES J. ROBERTS
On the Highroad of Surrender

Hope in Dependence

*"Then the glory of the LORD will be revealed,
and all flesh will see it together;
for the mouth of the LORD has spoken."*

ISAIAH 40:5 NASB

The Christian life is full of paradoxes, like this one: Only when we are totally dependent on our Redeemer are we truly free!

Carefully woven throughout chapters forty to sixty-six of Isaiah are specific portraits of Christ, presented by the names He called Himself throughout His ministry on earth. "Like a shepherd He will tend His flock, in His arm He will gather the lambs, and carry them in His bosom; He will gently lead the nursing ewes" (Isaiah 40:11 NASB).

Then we will see Him as the Counselor. "Who has directed the Spirit of the LORD, or as His counselor has informed Him?" (Isaiah 40:13 NASB)

We can know Him as Creator. "Do you not know? Have you not heard? The Everlasting God, the LORD, the Creator of the ends of the earth does not become weary or tired. His understanding is inscrutable" (Isaiah 40:28 NASB).

Jesus is the First and the Last. "Who has performed and accomplished it, calling forth the generations from the beginning? 'I, the LORD, am the first, and with the last. I am He'" (Isaiah 41:4 NASB). Christ clarifies this further in Revelation 1:8: "'I am the Alpha and the Omega,' says the Lord God, 'who is and who was and who is to come, the Almighty'" (NASB).

CAROL L. FITZPATRICK
Daily Wisdom for Women

Hopeful Trust

*Those who trust in the LORD are like Mount Zion,
which cannot be shaken but endures forever.*

<small>PSALM 125:1 NIV</small>

Does your job seem secure? Or are you constantly listening to gossip at the watercooler or Coke machine to discover the latest dirt about the corporate finances? Are things looking up for your company, or are they looking mighty grim?

Most of us expect our companies to provide security. We all want good, secure jobs. But when a company starts looking precarious, we worry about the future and may even start looking for another "good, secure job."

Our incomes keep us alive, so of course job security concerns us. We want to pay the rent and grocery bills and can't do it if we don't work. But when we place all our trust in companies, we'll experience disappointment. CEOs can't predict the financial future, hard as they try. Managers can't be certain our positions won't be axed in a corporate downsize.

But when we look to God for security, we will never be shaken. He knows the future. He foresees what jobs we need, long before we find them. Even if we lose our jobs unexpectedly, He helps us pay the rent and feed the kids.

Today, are you trusting in a short-term business or an eternal Father?

PAMELA MCQUADE
Daily Wisdom for the Workplace

The Dream List

Write the vision, and make it plain upon tables,
that he may run that readeth it.

HABAKKUK 2:2 KJV

Years ago, I made a list of things I wanted to do in my lifetime. It included things like sailing around the world, attending the Olympics, going on a cruise, and traveling Europe by train with my husband. I haven't accomplished all of them, and some I no longer have an interest in doing, like skydiving or hang gliding. (Those urges passed with the big hair of the 1980s.) Still, it's fun to review the list and see how many I've accomplished, which ones I no longer want to do, and others that are yet to be done. And of course, there are always new ones to add.

Writing down a vision—whether personal or professional—is a great way to keep your dreams in front of you. And as time passes, it's a great encouragement. During those times when you feel like you're going nowhere, your list can remind you of all that you've accomplished. Then you can thank God for giving you the desires of your heart, because He is the Author and Finisher of your life.

GENA MASELLI
Daily Wisdom for Working Women

Hope in Battle

"For the battle is not yours, but God's. . . . You will not have to fight this battle. Take up your positions; stand firm and see the deliverance the LORD will give you."

2 CHRONICLES 20:15, 17 NIV

I remember once, as my two-year-old son was running to me, he tripped over himself and fell. He hopped up and said, "Oops, I dropped myself." He didn't get discouraged in his efforts to walk; he accepted this as par for the course for someone his age. He didn't compare himself to me, but on occasion, he did ask me to help him along.

Each time I "dropped myself" spiritually, the devil left his calling card of discouragement. I was measuring my spiritual growth and progress by the beautiful Christian role models around me. I was becoming more and more despondent because I couldn't measure up, instead of simply accepting and acknowledging my limitations, as my little son had done, and asking for His help, which He would have lovingly and readily given.

I began to wake up to the realization that if I continued to try to live victoriously in my own strength, I could expect nothing but failure and discouragement. I began to see that I was expecting perfection. I was expecting more of myself than the Lord was expecting of me! I was trying to win the battles alone and was disappointed with myself when I lost. But the Lord doesn't expect us to fight alone. He says that He will go with us and fight for us.

GIGI GRAHAM TCHIVIDJIAN
A Quiet Knowing

Choreography of Hope

My own hand laid the foundations of the earth,
and my right hand spread out the heavens;
when I summon them, they all stand up together.

ISAIAH 48:13 NIV

Hardly a day goes by without my receiving a letter, a phone call, or a visit from someone in trouble. Almost always the question comes, in one form or another, *Why does God do this to me?*

When I am tempted to ask that same question, it loses its power when I remember that this Lord, into whose strong hands I long ago committed my life, is engineering a universe of unimaginable proportions and complexity. How could I possibly understand all that He must have taken into consideration as He deals with it and with me, a single individual! He has given us countless assurances that we cannot get lost in the shuffle. He choreographs the "molecular dance" which goes on every second of every minute of every day in every cell in the universe. For the record, one cell has about 200 trillion molecules. He makes note of the smallest seed and the tiniest sparrow. He is not too busy to keep records even of my falling hair.

Yet in our darkness we suppose He has over-looked us. He hasn't.

ELISABETH ELLIOT
Keep a Quiet Heart

Hope of Freedom

Therefore, there is now no condemnation for those who are in Christ Jesus, because through Christ Jesus the law of the Spirit of life set me free from the law of sin and death.

ROMANS 8:1–2 NIV

As I sat across from this young mother, listening to her story, my heart broke. The hand that life had dealt her, poor choices, lack of family support, and more contributed to the reason I was looking at her through a thick pane of glass. She was in jail, weeping for the children she left behind, uncertain of her future and feeling extremely alone.

Many of us are just like her. No, we may not have broken the law, but we live in our own prison of sorts. Emotionally, we chain ourselves to wrong thinking, believing lies of who we are. We are shackled by looming guilt or shame that keeps us

from moving forward and embracing the plans
God has for us. We have locked our hearts behind
a wall of protection so as not to get hurt by others
again. Some of us have never invited Jesus into our
lives while others of us who have, haven't followed
Him. Whatever the situation, there are many of us
who have experienced bondage.

There is hope for all of us. No matter what we
have done or how long we have been behind "bars,"
Jesus is inviting us to take His hand and follow
Him. Because of Jesus Christ, we don't have to live
in condemnation any longer. Jesus has unlocked the
prison door and set us free.

JOCELYN HAMSHER
Circle of Friends

A Vessel God Can Use

Many of the Samaritans from that town believed in him because of the woman's testimony, "He told me everything I ever did."

JOHN 4: 39 NIV

The Samaritan woman didn't have impressive credentials—spiritual, social, or otherwise—but she knew enough to listen to Jesus and to consider His claims upon her life. She didn't pretend to have all the right answers, but she was willing to pose the right questions. And she was willing to point people to Christ so they, too, could make their own decisions about His claims. She knew there was nothing within her that would "win people to Christ," nothing she could point to and say, "Hey, don't you want to be like me?"

What did she know? She knew she was a sinner who had met Jesus face-to-face. That was enough to transform her. She knew her past mistakes didn't matter. All that mattered was telling as many people as possible about Jesus. She wasn't a perfect woman, but she was a vessel God could use.

No matter who you are or what mistakes you've made, the most important thing you can know about yourself is whether or not you have encountered Christ. Let's rejoice in the knowledge that Jesus meets us right where we live and accepts us in whatever condition we come. What we did yesterday doesn't matter; it's the future that counts. If you will only believe, God can transform you into a vessel He can use.

DONNA PARTOW
Becoming a Vessel God Can Use

All Our Hope Is in God

For if Abraham was justified by works, he has something to boast about, but not before God. For what does the Scripture say? "Abraham believed God, and it was credited to him as righteousness."

ROMANS 4:2–3 NASB

Our work ethic is as old as the Garden of Eden. Because of sin Adam's free ride was over and he would now have to earn a living. But God said, "'Because you have listened to the voice of your wife, and have eaten from the tree about which I commanded you, saying, "You shall not eat from it"; cursed is the ground because of you; in toil you will eat of it all the days of your life'" (Genesis 3:17 NASB).

Somehow men and women have transferred this attitude about working for things to salvation. However, salvation is not based on our "goodness," but rather on Christ's. For no matter how diligently we try to keep those Ten Commandments, we're going to fail.

God made Abraham, the one the Jews claim as their father, a promise and he believed God. His belief wasn't merely an intellectual assent. The "Supreme God of the Universe," who made absolutely everything that Abraham now saw in his world, had deigned not only to speak to him, but He promised him an heir. The reason that Abraham could place his trust in God was because God kept His promises. No matter how impossible the situation looks, God always comes through.

CAROL L. FITZPATRICK
Daily Wisdom for Women

Hope in Trials, Part 1

It's best to stay in touch with both sides of an issue.
A person who fears God deals responsibly
with all of reality, not just a piece of it.

ECCLESIASTES 7:18 MSG

Frustrated and confused by the rumors surrounding the circumstances of our son Jason's arrest, I screamed out loud to my husband, Gene, "Don't people have anything else to do? They are getting a feeling of power out of announcing our bad news in the name of prayer requests, when they don't even have all the facts straight. This is so wrong!"

Gene is a unique personality. He never gets as animated as I do in the middle of an emotional outburst, nor does he "hit bottom" as far down as I do when things are not going well. He's steady, even, and controlled most of the time. Following my outburst that day, Gene took my hands in his two hands and said, "Carol, what's happened here is way out of our control. We are proactive people and we like to 'fix' things, but we can't change what's taken place or how people respond to it. There's not one thing we can do to stop the rumors, the stories, the opinions, and the gossiping of people. We have to let it go. This is way beyond us."

CAROL KENT
When I Lay My Isaac Down

Hope in Trials, Part 2

After all this, God tested Abraham. God said,
"Abraham!" "Yes?" answered Abraham.
"I'm listening." He said, "Take your dear son Isaac
whom you love and go to the land of Moriah.
Sacrifice him there as a burnt offering on one of
the mountains that I'll point out to you."

GENESIS 22:1–2 MSG

The first day I saw our son Jason in jail for the murder of his wife's ex-husband, I knew there was no way to fix things and make life as it was before. That day I took the first step in "laying my Isaac down." I admitted to God that I was helpless. I stood in the parking lot and cried until I ran out of tears. I physically opened up my hands, palm side up, and said:

"God, please help us not to waste this suffering.

I could not go on living if I didn't believe I could trust You even in this. I give up my right to control the outcome of Jason's trial. I release his future to Your keeping, but God, even while I'm saying I want to relinquish my control, I want to take it back. So God, I will let go of my control for the next minute, and if I make it that far, let's try for five more minutes, and maybe there will be a time when I will come to the end of one full day."

CAROL KENT
When I Lay My Isaac Down

Open Arms

I, even I, am He who blots out your transgressions for
My own sake; and I will not remember your sins.

ISAIAH 43:25 NKJV

I had my first car wreck when I was seventeen. I
was about an hour away from home, with a banged-
up car and a flat tire I didn't know how to change. I
had to make that dreaded phone call to my dad to
let him know what had happened. I'll never forget
that moment when I saw him pull into the parking
lot beside my wrecked car. I was so scared about
how he would respond, what he would say to me.
But as he walked toward me, his arms were out-
stretched and he embraced me in a huge hug.

I often remind myself of that moment when
thinking about approaching my heavenly Father
when I've done something wrong or stupid. When

I call on Him, admit what I've done, His response is like my dad's. He longs to embrace me and fix the mess I've made. Sure, there are consequences for my actions. But we have a Father who is loving and who is faithful and just to forgive us our sins when we confess them to Him. He wipes the slate clean and remembers our sin no more.

There's no reason to approach the throne of grace in fear, because it is a throne of *grace*. And when we find ourselves there broken over our sins, we are met with open arms.

EMILY SMITH
Circle of Friends

Hope in Jesus

I say unto you, that likewise joy shall be in heaven over one sinner that repenteth, more than over ninety and nine just persons, which need no repentance.

LUKE 15:7 KJV

Has God ever thrown a party for you? Do you know how much doing that would thrill Him?

When a soul enters eternity by faith in Jesus, all heaven rejoices over that new member of God's kingdom. You might say God throws a party just for the new believer. All heaven celebrates for each person who comes to God through His Son. If you know Jesus, there was a day when God gave a celebration with your name on it. Invitations went out to all heaven, and everyone had a great time rejoicing in what God had done in your life. It was a great day!

If you've never had such a great day in your

life, it can still happen. All you need to do is admit to God that you need to turn your life around. Tell Him you know you've sinned and need His forgiveness and that you're trusting in Jesus for that forgiveness.

Do I hear a party starting?

PAMELA McQUADE
Daily Wisdom for the Workplace

The Consecrated Life

Many are the plans in a man's heart,
but it is the LORD's purpose that prevails.

PROVERBS 19:21 NIV

Though one might hitch her "wagon to a star,"
so high and noble are her aspirations, yet if after all
that star is an earthly one—knowledge, personal influence, ability, riches, honor—and her aspirations
be realized and she arise high in the world, she will
not find the satisfaction in her attainments that she
hoped for. We, in our natures, are not altogether
earthly; there is in us a nature that craves to be in
tune with heaven. A life that gives exercise to this
part of our being and provides a way for the satisfy-
ing of the heart's craving for God is the only one
that brings what every person desires—soul rest.

This consecrated life is expected of every

Christian. In fact, no person can live a conscientious, Christian life long without finding such a consecration necessary. Either she must give herself fully to God, or drop back into the cold, formal life that many live, but none enjoy. Do not let anyone think that such a devoted life is irksome, for it is not. We are so created that the heart naturally craves God, and when the powers of sin that bind have been broken and the soul has been set free to follow its right course, the highest pleasure is found in sincere service to God.

MABEL HALE
Beautiful Girlhood

Worry No More

For the LORD will go before you.

ISAIAH 52:12 NIV

When I was a child struggling with my future, my grandmother gave me the "gift" of a worry stone. Holding this flat, oval-shaped, polished gemstone between her fingers and thumb, Grandma showed me how to rub the stone. She said that when I did this, I would gain relief from the concerns that plagued me.

As I grew, I used this worry stone when plagued by what-ifs. "What if I flunk this exam?" *Rub, rub. . .* I got a B. "What if Daddy should die?" *Rub, rub. . .* My father died on my sixteenth birthday. "What if Mark breaks up with me?" *Rub, rub. . . I* broke up with Mark.

As the years went by, I began to realize that it didn't matter how much I used the worry stone, because it changed neither the present nor the future. So I put the stone away. . .but kept the worries close at hand.

Then, years later, I visited the only church we have in Silverdale, Pennsylvania. And there, for the first time in my life, I connected with God in a personal, life-changing way. I began attending church and Sunday school every week and diving into God's Word with an unquenchable thirst.

As I read I discovered the powerful words of Jeremiah 29:11–12: " 'For I know the plans I have for you,' declares the LORD, 'plans to prosper you and not to harm you, plans to give you hope and a future. Then you will call upon me and come and pray to me, and I will listen to you' " (NIV).

I was awestruck. God had plans for me! Plans to prosper and not to harm me! Plans to give me hope and a future! I began to revel in this knowledge. I realized that when worries began to come upon me, all I had to do was call upon Him, seek Him with all my heart, and tell Him all my fears of the future. He would listen and then lead me to go in the power of His divine guidance, urging me to be confident that He is before me in the going. He's got a plan for my life, full of hope in and prosperity with Him, and He will give me the power to proceed!

DONNA K. MALTESE
Power Prayers to Start Your Day

Hope in Resurrection

"For God so loved the world that he gave his one and only Son, that whoever believes in him shall not perish but have eternal life."

JOHN 3:16 NIV

We have a man down on the play," the announcer said during the Friday night high school football game in Rose Hill, North Carolina.

LuAnn watched helplessly as her son collapsed on the field and didn't get up. After a few moments she rushed from the stands and held Will in her arms as he took his last breath. A concussion of the heart, the doctors explained later.

O God, how can a mother bear the loss of her precious son? I prayed.

Then He reminded me of Mary, who watched her son, battered and bleeding, nailed to a cruel Roman cross.

"Yes, Lord," I said. "But Jesus came back to life. Will won't."

I kept my questioning to myself, knowing it wouldn't help anyone.

A few days later, LuAnn courageously spoke at her son's funeral. She stood before a crowded congregation and told about Jesus, whom Will loved.

"Accept Jesus as your Savior and receive eternal life," she urged.

Thirty people came to faith that day.

The following week LuAnn spoke at the opponent's school assembly. Again she shared the gospel, and many boys and girls came to Christ.

It was an extraordinary moment when I realized that while Will was not physically raised from the dead, resurrection power took place as hundreds of souls experienced new life in Christ through his story.

SHARON JAYNES
Extraordinary Moments with God

Let Go

So do not fear, for I am with you; do not be dismayed,
for I am your God. I will strengthen you and help
you; I will uphold you with my righteous right hand.

ISAIAH 41:10 NIV

$\mathcal{D}$o you recollect the delicious sense of rest with which you have sometimes gone to bed at night, after a day of great exertion and weariness? How delightful was the sensation of relaxing every muscle and letting your body go in a perfect abandonment of ease and comfort! The strain of the day had ceased, for a few hours at least, and the work of the day had been laid off. You no longer had to hold up an aching head or a weary back. You trusted yourself to the bed in an absolute confidence, and it held you up, without effort, or strain, or even thought, on your part. You rested!

But suppose you had doubted the strength or

the stability of your bed and had dreaded each moment to find it giving way beneath you and landing you on the floor; would you have rested then? Would not every muscle hate been strained in a fruitless effort to hold yourself *up,* and would not the weariness have been greater than if you had not gone to bed at all?

Let this analogy teach you what it means to rest in the Lord. Let your souls lie down upon the couch of His sweet will, as your bodies lie down in their beds at night. Relax every strain, and lay off every burden. Let yourself go in a perfect abandonment of ease and comfort, sure that, since He holds you up, you are perfectly safe. Your part is simply to rest. His part is to sustain you; and He cannot fail.

HANNAH WHITALL SMITH
The Christian's Secret of a Happy Life

Step into Your Dreams

*This resurrection life you received from God is not a
timid, grave-tending life. It's adventurously expectant,
greeting God with a childlike "What's next, Papa?"*

ROMANS 8:15 MSG

In the early 1950s, Lillian Vernon spent five
hundred dollars on her first advertisement, offering
monogrammed belts and handbags. That one ad
produced a $32,000 profit! Today—more than fifty
years later—Lillian Vernon is still selling gift items
through a very successful catalog sales program. In
fact, her company now generates more than $250
million in sales every year.

But what if Lillian Vernon hadn't run that
small ad? What if she hadn't taken that risk? Well,
she wouldn't be a millionaire, and lots of folks
would have to find another catalog to use for their
annual Christmas shopping.

Maybe God has put a dream in your heart that

is so big you haven't even shared it with anyone. So what's stopping you? Why aren't you running that ad like Lillian Vernon?

If you're like most women, fear is holding you back. Fear is a very real emotion. It can get a grip on you that won't let go—until you make it let go through the Word of God. Say out loud, "I can do all things through Christ who strengthens me. I am the head and not the tail. I am more than a conqueror."

Remind yourself of who you are in Christ Jesus on a daily basis. God has crowned you with His favor. So grab hold of God's promises, put fear behind you, and step into your dreams. Pretty soon, you'll be sharing your success story!

MICHELLE MEDLOCK ADAMS
Secrets of Beauty

Your Song Is Coming

"My food," said Jesus "is to do the will of him who sent me and to finish his work."

JOHN 4:34 NIV

After being a Christian more than thirty years, the truth was I wasn't able to handle everything on my plate, but I was making myself sick trying. I thought God would take me through, but this time was different. I just wanted to cry and run away from life. I'd thought I was a maturing Christian, but now I wasn't so sure. How could I be and feel this way?

Did you know it's entirely possible to be desperately thirsty in body, mind, and spirit and not know it? I've hardly met a woman who hasn't been there at least once.

Jesus experienced deep thirst, too. He was thirsty to do the will of God, something otherworldly. Thirsty to bring His Father praise and honor and worship, to bring songs of joy to the throne of God. Not even His disciples knew what that meant until later.

We aren't born with that kind of thirst. We're reborn with it. The greatest joy in our journey toward renewal is recovering our thirst for God's glory, our own song of praise to Him.

You may not feel ready to sing anything today. No one does when she is flat-out. Add a dose of depression to the mix, and you have one songless canary. For now, know that your song is coming. It is unique to you, a special gift from God.

VIRELLE KIDDER
Meet Me at the Well

Always Sunshine

*So we fix our eyes not on what is seen, but on
what is unseen. For what is seen is temporary,
but what is unseen is eternal.*

2 Corinthians 4:18 niv

There is never a moment when I am absent
from the scene of your life. Your feeling of separation does not make it so. It is like the sunshine.
Clouds enshroud the earth and you say the sun
is not shining. This is not true. The sun is *always*
shining. The truth is that because it is a cloudy day,
you cannot *see* the sun shining. Even so, My grace
is always pouring down upon you, and in moments
when your own spirit may not discern it, My love is
nonetheless constant and real.

Rejoice in Me, for truly I am all you need. I am
light and life, hope and peace. I am the joy-giver.

My presence is with you, and wherever I am, there is harmony. I am your deliverer and the source of all your strength. You can never ask beyond My power to provide.

Your joy may be restored at any moment as you brush aside the clouds of earth by recapturing the strength of the times when you have felt the warmth of the sunshine, yes, even been blinded by the power of its rays.

FRANCES J. ROBERTS
On the Highroad of Surrender

Choosing Hope

Though you have made me see troubles, many and bitter, you will restore my life again; from the depths of the earth you will again bring me up.

PSALM 71:20 NIV

When I was six weeks of age a slight cold caused an inflammation of the eyes, which appeared to demand the attention of the family physician; but he not being at home, a stranger was called. He recommended the use of hot poultices, which ultimately destroyed the sense of sight. When this sad misfortune became known throughout our neighborhood, the unfortunate man thought it best to leave; and we never heard of him again. But I have not for a moment, in more than eighty-five years, felt a spark of resentment against him because I have always believed from my youth to this very moment that the good Lord, in His Infinite Mercy, by this means consecrated me to the work that I am still permitted to do. When I remember His mercy and loving-kindness; when I have been blessed above the common lot of mortals; and when happiness has touched the deep places of my soul, how can I repine? "The light of the body is the eye; if, therefore, thine eye be single thy whole body shall be full of light. But if thine eye be evil, thy whole body shall be full of darkness. If, therefore, the light that is in thee be darkness, how great is that darkness!"

FANNY CROSBY
Memories of Eighty Years

The Sweetness of
Little Flowers

He has scattered abroad his gifts to the poor,
his righteousness endures forever;
his horn will be lifted high in honor.

PSALM 112:9 NIV

For a long time I wondered why God showed partiality, why all souls don't receive the same amount of graces. I was astounded to see Him lavish extraordinary favors on the Saints who had offended Him such as St. Paul and St. Augustine, and whom He so to speak forced to receive His graces. Or when I read the life of Saints whom Our Lord was pleased to embrace from the cradle to the grave; without leaving in their path any obstacles that might hinder them from rising toward Him, and granting these souls such favors that they were unable to tarnish the immaculate brightness of their baptismal robes, I wondered: why poor primitive people, for example, were dying in great numbers without even having heard the name of God pronounced.

Jesus consented to teach me this mystery. He placed before my eyes the book of nature; I understood that all the flowers that He created are beautiful. The brilliance of the rose and the whiteness of the lily don't take away the perfume of the lowly violet or the delightful simplicity of the daisy. . . . I understood that if all the little flowers wanted to be roses, nature would lose its springtime adornment, and the fields would no longer be sprinkled with little flowers.

So it is in the world of souls, which is Jesus' garden. He wanted to create great saints who could be compared to lilies and roses. But He also created little ones, and these ought to be content to be daisies or violets destined to gladden God's eyes when He glances down at His feet. Perfection consists in doing His will, in being what He wants us to be.

SAINT THERESE OF LISIEUX
The Story of a Soul

Jesus, Our Lifeline

The name of the LORD is a strong fortress;
the godly run to him and are safe.

PROVERBS 18:10 NLT

The greatest moment of your life can be when everything seems finished for you. That is the moment when you lay your weak hand in the strong hand of Jesus. For Jesus can make life and death—present and future—victorious! He can give you eternal life; not only life in heaven, but life right now.

It is as when you have fallen in the sea and you think, *Now I will surely drown. I can swim perhaps an hour, but then I will sink!* A lifeline is the only thing that can help you then.

I found that when you are drowning in the terrific misery of the world, Jesus is everything for you—your only lifeline. When you think you have lost everything, then you can be *found* by Jesus Christ.

He died for you, He lives for you, and He loves you more than any human being can love. I have told people about Him for thirty-three years, in sixty-four countries, and in all that time nobody has ever told me he was sorry he asked Jesus to come into his life. You won't be sorry either.

CORRIE TEN BOOM
Oh, How He Loves You

Not Enough to Go Around

Cast thy burden upon the Lord, and he shall sustain thee: he shall never suffer the righteous to be moved.

PSALM 55:22 KJV

Did you ever walk on a balance beam when you were a child? I loved gymnastics when I was growing up, but I was never very good on the balance beam. I'd topple off to one side quite often. You know what's ironic? I'm still having trouble with that whole balancing concept. Only now I'm having trouble balancing my personal and professional life. How about you? Maybe you're an employee, a wife, a mom, a friend, a daughter, a sister, an aunt, a church volunteer, etc. And you're not sure how to be all of those things at one time. If you are all those things, welcome to the Sisterhood—the "Sisterhood of There's Not Enough of Me to Go Around."

There are days when I wonder how I am supposed to accomplish everything that is on my plate. But you know what? *I'm* not! God never intended me to do this by myself. And He never intended for you to go it alone, either. The Word tells us that we can do all things through Christ who gives us strength. All means all, right?

So no matter how many roles you're fulfilling today, don't sweat it! God will help you.

MICHELLE MEDLOCK ADAMS
Daily Wisdom for Working Women

Claiming God's Promise

And the LORD spake unto Moses, saying,
The daughters of Zelophehad speak right: thou shalt
surely give them a possession of an inheritance among
their father's brethren; and thou shalt cause the
inheritance of their father to pass unto them.

NUMBERS 27:6–7 KJV

What confidence the five daughters of Zelophehad had in God's provisions for women! Imagine the courage required for them to ask their leaders to deviate from established legal tradition as they petitioned: "Why should the name of our father be removed from among his family because he had no son? Give us a possession among our father's brothers" (Numbers 27:4 NKJV).

The laws God gave to the Hebrews were essential in maintaining law and order in the community and the property rights for individuals. This was crucial in ensuring that a family endured and prospered. Normally, such property passed through the sons.

Zelophehad was a descendant of Joseph, making his lineage vital to the community. While he died without sons, he did leave behind five daughters. According to existing law, Zelophehad's possessions were to pass to his brothers. Instead, these five women stepped out and appealed to Moses so that their father's lineage could continue.

When Moses then turned to God for an answer, the Lord agreed with Zelophehad's daughters: "If a man dies and has no son, then you shall cause his inheritance to pass to his daughter" (Numbers 27:8 NKJV). Only if a man had no children would his brothers inherit. In a patriarchal society in which women had few rights, this was a radical change. This God-dictated shift in Hebrew law reveals how much He cares for women.

RAMONA RICHARDS
Secrets of Confidence

Renewed Hope

*Answer me, GOD; O answer me and reveal to
this people that you are GOD, the true God.*

1 KINGS 18:37 MSG

Immediately after God opened a major door of
ministry for Elijah, he got new instructions. "God
then told Elijah, Get out of here, and fast. Head
east and hide out at the Kerith Ravine. . . . You can
drink fresh water from the brook; I've ordered the
ravens to feed you. . . . Elijah obeyed God's orders."
But after a while, "the brook dried up" (summary of
1 Kings 17:2–7).

Did you get that? After what appeared to be a
big-time opportunity for powerful and visible ministry, God sent Elijah to the brook—but it dried up.
It shut down. It quit meeting his needs. It left him
thirsty.

When the brook dries up, dreams shatter.
Hopes are dashed. God seems far away. We feel

abandoned by people we were hoping would satisfy our needs. But more than that, we feel rejected by a God who should have intervened in our situation. The One who is Living Water and says He loves us and wants to meet our needs has allowed the brook to dry up.

But the end of the story reminds us that it is never too late to resolve our fear in a God-honoring way. As we experience the deep *sorrow* of rejection and abandonment, our *brokenness* before God leads to a *surrender* of our stubborn, self-reliant will and paves the road for future *faith-filled decisions* that bring healing, acceptance, and nonpossessive love.

CAROL KENT
Tame Your Fears

He's Always There

Where can I go from your Spirit? Where can I flee from your presence? If I go up to the heavens, you are there; if I make my bed in the depths, you are there.

PSALM 139:7–8 NIV

"I won't leave you," I gently promised my young son for about the fifth time. A haphazard glance around the playground had just terrified him into thinking I had gone without him and he desperately needed my reassurance. "I am right here," I told him again and again when he continued to cling to me. I stifled an impatient sigh. How many times did I need to tell him the same thing? Why didn't he believe me? Suddenly, the irony hit me. What I was saying to my son sounded incredibly familiar. How many times does my God tell me *He* won't leave *me*? And how many times do I stubbornly ignore His reassurances?

In His Word, God tells me over and over that

He will not leave me. "'I will never leave you nor forsake you,'" He lovingly reminds me in Joshua 1:5. "For the Lord loves the just and will not forsake his faithful ones," He says again in Psalm 37:28. And when I cry out to Him again to make sure He's still there, He patiently directs me to Psalm 37:25: "I have never seen the righteous forsaken or their children begging bread." I have to reluctantly admit that I am more like a six-year-old than I would like to be. I, too, need to be continually reminded that God is right here beside me.

JANINE MILLER
Circle of Friends

Let's Make a Deal

*"But if serving the LORD seems
undesirable to you, then choose for
yourselves this day whom you will serve."*

JOSHUA 24:15 NIV

Let's Make a Deal! Remember the game show?
One popular game of suspense that occurred
frequently on the show was when a contestant was
asked to choose one of three doors without knowing what was concealed behind it. After vacillating
back and forth, the decision was made and the
contestant anxiously waited to see what was behind
the door. Sometimes it would be a new car received
with great enthusiasm. At other times, the outcome
was a hoax met with a disappointing sigh.

What if you were told you could choose one of
three doors but unlike the contestant on the game
show, you were told what's behind each one. Would
you do it? Read on.

Behind door one—your past. You can continue to let past abuse, broken relationships, or previous failures keep you held back and tied down. Or, you can break free of the past and choose something different like:

Door two—the present. You can choose to focus on the present and get caught up in all this world has to offer. You can pursue wealth, popularity, fun, and excitement. This present world has a lot to offer. "Is there something else to consider?" you ask. Yes. It's behind door three!

Door three—God and His plan for you. "Really? Does God really have something unique in mind for me?" The answer is yes. He has a dream for you to pursue. The choice is up to you.

BOBBIE RILL
Circle of Friends

Waiting in Hope

Wait on the LORD; be of good courage, and He shall strengthen your heart; wait, I say, on the LORD!

PSALM 27:14 NKJV

It's taken me decades to realize that waiting is more a posture of the heart than tapping my foot over the passage of time. It's willingness to yield to the One who loves me most, bowing to His Lordship—a requirement for learning anything deeper about God. Always open to our cry, the King of heaven is never in a hurry and expects to be trusted. His answers are always best, perfectly on time, and are worlds better than anything I could have imagined on my own.

We have friends who wait today while cancer's tentacles claim a spouse, or a tumor expands inside a son-in-law's head, or a beloved child changes course in sexual orientation or waits in a prison cell. What are they to do? How does any child of God wait quietly while the guillotine seems poised above?

Perhaps by grace. Perhaps by exhausting every repentant thought, every prayer for change. Then what remains is to lay our head on His lap and rest in His care. "Though he slay me, yet will I hope in him," said Job at a similar moment (13:15). Only by grace is quietness and confidence our strength— and only when His strange and holy Presence takes over completely. Such submission is not learned in seasons of blessing, but when every alternative is gone, we find He is enough, and His way is best.

VIRELLE KIDDER
The Best Life Ain't Easy, But It's Worth It

Hope in Endurance

*No discipline seems pleasant at the time,
but painful. Later on, however, it produces
a harvest of righteousness and peace for
those who have been trained by it.*

HEBREWS 12:11 NIV

My child, do not flinch under My disciplines. I never send more than you can endure, but often I know that is more than you think. Can you accept the cup of suffering as readily as you embrace joy? You can do so in greater degrees as your trust in Me increases. If you know I only send what is for your good, you will see all things good and will know it passes through My love as it comes to you.

Through much tribulation I am bringing My chosen to perfection. Be not amazed when challenges present themselves. I am building your fortitude, and the day will come when you will be grateful for every lesson learned in the school of affliction.

My love never fails, even when it brings you pain. My love endures all things (1 Corinthians 13:7) and it will teach you to do likewise. It is in the patient endurance of affliction that the soul is seasoned with grace. It is a barren life that holds only happiness. Saints are not nurtured by levity. Hope does not spring from good fortune.

Hold sacred *every experience*.

Frances J. Roberts
On the Highroad of Surrender

Unwavering Hope

But Jesus immediately said to them: "Take courage!
It is I. Don't be afraid." "Lord, if it's you," Peter
replied, "tell me to come to you on the water." "Come,"
he said. Then Peter got down out of the boat, walked
on the water and came toward Jesus. But when he
saw the wind, he was afraid and, beginning to sink,
cried out, "Lord, save me!" Immediately Jesus reached
out his hand and caught him. "You of little faith,"
he said, "why did you doubt?"

MATTHEW 14:27–31 NIV

Before this event occurred, Peter had already
seen Jesus heal a leper, mute demoniacs, his own
mother-in-law, and more. He'd even been present
when Jesus demonstrated His power over nature
by calming the wind. Still, after witnessing all these
miracles, Peter wavered on the water. Why? E. M.
Bounds provides this answer: "Doubt and fear are
the twin foes of faith."

Knowing this disciple would eventually sink,

why did Jesus invite him out of the boat? Matthew Henry writes, "Christ bid [Peter to] come, not only that he might walk upon the water, and so know Christ's power, but that he might sink, and so know his own weakness."

Knowing that even Peter doubted at times provides us with a little relief. Again, Matthew Henry writes: "The strongest faith and the greatest courage have a mixture of fear. Those that can say, *Lord, I believe*; must say, *Lord, help my unbelief.*"

Like Peter, when we begin to panic and find ourselves sinking, we must cry out in specific and fervent prayer to Jesus, saying, "Lord, save me!" And as Jesus did with Peter, He will *immediately* reach out and save us.

By keeping our eyes off our difficulties and fixed on Jesus, we will overcome our doubts and fears and find ourselves walking on the living water of His power, His Word, and His promises. We must be unwavering in our faith that God will uphold us no matter what our trial.

DONNA K. MALTESE
Power Prayers to Start Your Day

Accepting Truth

"Forget about what's happened; don't keep going over old history. Be alert, be present. I'm about to do something brand-new. It's bursting out! Don't you see it? There it is! I'm making a road through the desert, rivers in the badlands."

ISAIAH 43:18–19 MSG

Not only by the grace of God can we accept what is true about our past, but in Christ our very wounds and scars can be redeemed. Pain is hard; there's no doubt. But pain reminds us why Christ died. It reminds us to bring our wounds to the wounded Healer so He can make us better. In turn, we can comfort others as we have been comforted and look to a future free from hurt. We are not asked to pretend our wounds don't exist, but to let go and stop holding on to them so tightly.

Being set free from the past means accepting what is true, not what we wish was true. Sometimes we have to make peace with what was or is to be able to let go and move on. So many of us put ourselves in situations to be hurt over and over by the same person because we know things *should* be different. We cling to our dreams of what we wish the past could have been and set ourselves up to be hurt again and again. If this is you, I encourage you to let go of that past—your "what should have been"—and embrace your "what is" and your "what can be." Truth is powerful. At times it is heartbreaking, but ultimately, it will deliver you.

Sheila Walsh
Let Go

Experiencing Happily Ever After

So put on all the armor that God gives.
Then when that evil day comes, you will
be able to defend yourself. And when the
battle is over, you will still be standing firm.

Ephesians 6:13 cev

Have you ever noticed that in a fairy tale there's usually a damsel in distress? She dreams about the day a valiant knight on his white horse will ride up to the castle, slay the dragon, use the alligators as stepping-stones, climb up the tower, and rescue her.

Maybe you've had that dream yourself. Well, stop dreaming, sister! Your dream has already come true, and it's heavenly! Your Prince (the Prince of Peace) has already come on His white horse. And He didn't just rescue you. He also took away your victim status and made you into a victor! He even gave you armor—the full armor of God—to protect you as you fight evil.

Sure, fairy tales are fun to watch on the big screen, but I don't want to be a damsel in distress in real life. A princess—yes. A damsel in distress—no. God doesn't want you to be a damsel in distress, either. If you've been living with a victim's mentality for too long, it's time to wise up to the Word. The Word says that we can use God's mighty weapons to knock down the devil's strongholds.

Your damsel-in-distress days are behind you. You are a beautiful princess—a member of God's royal family. And if you've made Jesus the Lord of your life, you are promised an eternity of "happily ever after."

MICHELLE MEDLOCK ADAMS
Secrets of Beauty

Confident Hope

And Deborah, a prophetess, the wife of Lapidoth,
she judged Israel at that time.

JUDGES 4:4 KJV

Throughout scripture, the faith women had in God provides them with the confidence to stand up for their beliefs. One woman is even called to guide ten thousand men into battle.

The only woman to sit as a judge over Israel, Deborah already had a strong relationship with the Lord when she was called to sit as judge for Israel at a time of harsh oppression. Yet in a society that did not always value women as leaders, she answered God's call on her life.

Using her wisdom to settle disputes for her people, however, is a far cry from leading them into battle against an army featuring nine hundred iron chariots. Jabin, the king in Canaan, had dealt harshly with the Israelites for more than twenty years, using his army to keep them under his rule.

Finally, they cried out to God for relief in what appeared to be an impossible situation to overcome.

Deborah, however, had the ability to see beyond the current situation. She called on Barak to do as the Lord had commanded, to take his troops and prepare to face Sisera, Jabin's general, in a battle to save their people. Barak's response—that he would do so only if she was with him—underscores the trust Israel had placed in the woman God had called for them.

God looks for women who are ready to embrace His vision. Such women of vision have the courage that enables them to conquer and overcome in situations that would otherwise seem unconquerable.

RAMONA RICHARDS
Secrets of Confidence

Hope Conquers Fear

And they who know Your name [who have experience
and acquaintance with Your mercy] will lean on and
confidently put their trust in You, for You, Lord, have
not forsaken those who seek (inquire of and for) You.

PSALM 9:10 AMP

Fear comes in many sizes, shapes, and forms.

As Christians, how do we face fear?

When fear invades our spirits, we need to turn to the One in whom we have confidence—Jesus Christ. The One who tells us that He is with us always, "to the very end of the age" (Matthew 28:20 NIV).

Although we may not understand why certain things happen in our lives, God instructs us to be courageous, for "no one will be able to stand up against you all the days of your life. . . . I will be with you; I will never leave you nor forsake you" (Joshua 1:5 NIV). Do you have this confidence—that God is with you in the storms of life?

David wrote of his trust in God in many of the Psalms, most notably, Psalm 23: "I will fear no evil, for you are with me" (verse 4 NIV).

The only confidence we have in this life is knowing that God is always with us. And if we are wise enough, we will look for and find God in every moment, filled with the assurance that He is with us through the good and the bad. If we follow God—through prayer and the application of His Word—He will keep us close to Him, traveling down the right path, until we reach our home, where He greets us.

DONNA K. MALTESE
Power Prayers to Start Your Day

Hope in the Advocate

"And I will ask the Father, and he will give you another Counselor to be with you forever—the Spirit of truth."

JOHN 14:16–17 NIV

*D*uring Jesus' Last Supper discourse, He reassured the disciples that He would not leave them as orphans. The Greek word here for "counselor," which is also translated *Helper* (NASB) and *Comforter* (KJV) is *parakletos* and means a "person summoned to one's aid." Originally it was a term used in a court of justice to denote a legal assistant, counsel for the defense, an advocate; then, generally, one who pleads another's cause, an intercessor, an advocate.

I love the image of being in a court of law because I have come to see Satan as the "accuser of our brethren" (Revelation 12:10 NASB). He points his gnarly finger in our faces and says things like, "You aren't a very good Christian," "Jesus doesn't really love you," "You were a mistake when you were born," "You've really blown it this time," "I don't see much fruit in your life," "You're a pitiful excuse as a wife, as a mother, as a child of God." Have you ever heard any of those statements before? Perhaps you've always assumed these were your own musings. I believe those accusatory statements are words from Satan that he whispers in our ears.

On the other hand, the Holy Spirit is our counselor, our attorney, the one who comes alongside us and repeats, "Not guilty! Not guilty! Not guilty!" He says, "You, My child, have been set free! Your debt has been paid in full."

SHARON JAYNES
Becoming a Woman Who Listens to God

Never Uncomfortable

My eyes fail, looking for your promise; I say,
"When will you comfort me?"

PSALM 119:82 NIV

Our Comforter is not far off in Heaven where we cannot find Him. He is close at hand. He abides with us. When Christ was going away from this earth, He told His disciples that He would not leave them comfortless, but would send "another Comforter" who would abide with them forever. This Comforter, He said, would teach them all things, and would bring all things to their remembrance. And then He declared as though it were the necessary result of the coming of this divine Comforter: "Peace I leave with you, my peace I *give* unto you; not as the world giveth, give I unto you. Let not your 'heart [therefore] be troubled, neither let it be afraid." Oh, how can we, in the face of these tender and loving words, go about with troubled and frightened hearts?

"Comforter"—what a word of bliss, if we only could realize it. Let us repeat it over and over to ourselves, until its meaning sinks into the very depths of our being. And an "abiding" Comforter, too, not one who comes and goes, and is never on hand when most needed, but one who is always present, and always ready to give us "joy for mourning, and the garment of praise for the spirit of heaviness."

If we can have a human comforter to stay with us for only a few days when we are in trouble, we think ourselves fortunate; but here is a divine Comforter who is always staying with us, and whose power to comfort is infinite. Never, never ought we for a single minute to be without comfort; never for a single minute ought we to be uncomfortable.

HANNAH WHITALL SMITH
The God of All Comfort

Hope in the Truth

But if we walk in the light, as he is in the light,
we have fellowship with one another, and the
blood of Jesus, his Son, purifies us from all sin.

1 JOHN 1:7 NIV

As a child, I suffered a crippling fear of the dark. Monsters crouched under my bed and in the closet. Only a wedge of light from the living room held them at bay, along with my nightly ritual recitation of the Lord's Prayer. Another terrifying door led from my bedroom to the hundred-and-fifty-year-old stone basement in our small house. From the age of six, I practiced locking it tightly before going to bed.

Other fears held me fast, too, things I didn't talk about. With my father's mental illness and disappearance when I was seven, followed by his death a few years later, death became my greatest fear of all, not my own, but the horrible fear that my mother or older brother might die as well.

As I became an adult, I found that fears don't go away. They just change masks and whisper low growling threats from their hiding place. What if my child dies? Or my husband? Does God care about me? Is He even real?

He heard.

There came a day, bright as the morning, when new friends grasped my hand and walked me toward the Light. With their help, I placed my trust in Jesus, the Truth I'd long sought, the Way to my real Father, God. In His presence darkness cannot exist, fear loses its death grip, and His forever Love set me free.

VIRELLE KIDDER

The Dance of the Delighted

"The Lord your God is with you, he is mighty to save.
He will take great delight in you, he will quiet you
with his love, he will rejoice over you with singing."

ZEPHANIAH 3:17 NIV

My youngest nephew, who is seven, is mad about guinea pigs. I spent one evening hanging out with John Michael while he frolicked with his furry friends. He danced in circles around them, "chatted" nose to nose with them, and stretched out on the floor so the pseudo-rats could scurry around on his tummy. The entire time, he kept erupting into contagious giggles!

My nephew wasn't doing anything particularly praiseworthy, he was simply doing what he loves to do. It's taken me a very long time to believe that

God delights in me, even when I'm just *being me*. I used to think God was a stern taskmaster and the only time He was pleased with me was when I was doing something "religious," like volunteering with children's Sunday school or teaching the Bible at a women's conference. Basically I thought He loved me out of *duty*—because it was written in His divine job description. The concept of God's *delighting* in me seemed as plausible as pigs flying.

But this petite book named after a minor prophet actually records that eye-popping promise. Even though God's people were behaving badly, even though they deserved a big fat spanking, our merciful Creator chose to sing lyrics of restoration. Instead of knocking them across the room, He crooned a love song. And that kind of music makes me feel like dancing!

LISA HARPER
What the Bible Is All About for Women

I Have Planned
Ahead for You

Nevertheless I am continually with You;
You have taken hold of my right hand.
With Your counsel You will guide me.

PSALM 73:23–24 NASB

Behold, am I a God that is afar off, and not a
God that is near? For in the midst of difficulties,
I will be your support. In the darkness, I am your
Light; there is no darkness that can hide My face
from the eye of faith. My beauty and My radiance
are all the lovelier in darkness.

In grief, My comfort is more poignant. In
failure, My encouragement the most welcome. In
loneliness, the touch of My presence more tender.
You are hidden in Me, and I will multiply both
the wisdom and the strength in due proportion to
meet the demands of every occasion.

I am the Lord your God. I know no limitations.

I know no lack. I need not reserve My stores, for
I always have a fresh supply. You can by no means
ever exhaust My infinite resources. Let your heart
run wild. Let your imagination go vagabond. No
extravagance of human thought can ever plumb
the depths of My planning and provision for My
children.

Rejoice, therefore, and face each day with joy;
for I have planned ahead for you, and made all
necessary arrangements and reservations. I am your
guide and benefactor. Put your hand in Mine.

FRANCES J. ROBERTS
Come Away My Beloved

Choose Faith

Don't be afraid, because I am your God.
I will make you strong and will help you; I will
support you with my right hand that saves you.

ISAIAH 41:10 NCV

I have never met a woman who has not struggled at some level with the fear of success or the fear of failure. One woman wrote, "I have desperately wanted everyone, anyone, or someone to think I was wonderful, talented, exciting, and spiritual." This woman's self-esteem was so fragile due to past issues that she was in bondage to the fear of failure.

On the other hand, some of us are over-whelmed by the secret fear that to be successful, we must do something so spectacular that the whole world will validate our worth. When we get caught up in this philosophy, we often *do* accomplish something worthy of applause, but often the fear of failure looms in the background because of the personal sacrifices that have allowed the success.

Much of our fear centers on being unable to identify what will bring a sense of purpose, joy, and fulfillment to our lives. Fear of making the wrong choice in our life's work. Fear of getting trapped in dead-end marriages and/or vocations. Fear of *not* having children. Fear of *having* children and being bad parents. Fear of trying something new because we've never succeeded in the past.

The opposite of fear is faith. Fear makes us withdraw and hide behind our escape mechanisms. Fear exposes our disappointments and makes us choose a rigid or a yielding resolution for those fears. Faith or fear? The choice is ours.

CAROL KENT
Tame Your Fears

Heaven Is No Dream

Thy mercy, O Lord, is in the heavens;
and thy faithfulness reacheth unto the clouds.

<small>PSALM 36:5 KJV</small>

This evening the clouds lay low on the mountains, so that sometimes we could hardly see them, and sometimes the stars were nearly all covered. But always, just when it seemed as though the mountains were going to be quite lost in the mist, the higher peaks pushed out, and whereas the dimmer stars were veiled, the brighter ones shone through. Even supposing the clouds had wholly covered the face of the mountains, and not a star had shone through the piled-up masses, the mountains would still have stood steadfast, and the stars would not have ceased to shine.

I thought of this and found it very comforting, simple as it is. Our feelings do not affect God's facts. They may blow up like clouds and cover the eternal things that we do most truly believe. We may not see the shining of the promises, but still they shine; and the strength of the hills that is His also, is not for one moment less because of our human weakness.

Heaven is no dream. Feelings go and come like clouds, but the hills and the stars abide.

AMY CARMICHAEL
Edges of His Ways

Death Conqueror

"The thief does not come except to steal, and to kill, and to destroy. I have come that they may have life, and that they may have it more abundantly."

JOHN 10:10 NKJV

When Jesus died on the cross, He also rose from the dead to break the power of death over anyone who receives His life. Jesus conquered death—whether at the end of our lives or in the multiple ways that we face death daily. In the death of our dreams, finances, health, or relationships, Jesus can bring His life to resurrect those dead places in us. Therefore we don't have to feel hopeless.

He also gives to everyone who opens up to Him a quality of life that is meaningful, abundant, and fulfilling. He transcends our every limitation and boundary and enables us to do things we never would have been capable of aside from Him. He is the only one with power and authority over the emotions or bondage that torture us. He is the only one who can give us life before death as well as life hereafter.

Without Him we die a little every day. With Him we become more and more alive.

STORMIE OMARTIAN
Praying God's Will for Your Life

Quiet Beauty

Let it be the hidden person of the heart, with the incorruptible beauty of a gentle and quiet spirit, which is very precious in the sight of God.

1 PETER 3:4 NKJV

Silver-haired and sixtyish, Elizabeth radiated stylish poise and unflappable acceptance of others. Her husband, Fred, was a quiet man, likeable but not much for socializing. Whenever he came to church, they amazed me by often holding hands, and I'd think to myself, *That's the kind of marriage I wish we could have someday.*

One day I confided my deep loneliness at home and the terrible longing I felt for Steve to share my faith.

"I know how you feel, Virelle," she answered, leveling those beautiful gray-blue eyes at me. "I've been praying for Fred for forty years."

"What?" I blurted out my amazement. "How

have you lasted that long? How come you both seem so happy?"

"I learned one day that God called me to love Fred, to honor him, and make his life as happy as I possibly could. He never asked me to change him. Only someone as big and as powerful as God can change a husband!"

And He did. I learned many years later that Fred received Christ as Savior shortly before his death. What made Elizabeth so beautiful? It had to be her loving heart, one that ruled her tongue, her facial expressions, her voice, her touch, her time. She was the evidence I needed, the perfect visual of a Christ-filled life. I wanted to become like that, no matter what it took.

VIRELLE KIDDER
The Best Life Ain't Easy, But It's Worth It

Hope for Unanswered Questions

*Why are you in despair, O my soul? And why
have you become disturbed within me? Hope in God,
for I shall yet praise Him, the help of my
countenance and my God.*

PSALM 42:11 NASB

No matter what the pain and problems may be
like, everybody is looking for the answers to two
basic questions: WHY? and HOW? Folks who write
to me often ask, "Why me?" "Why us?" "Why our
family?" But just as often they also want to know,
"How?" "How can I deal with this?" "How do I
learn to live with pain?"

I don't have all the answers. Frankly, sometimes
I'm not even sure I fully understand the questions.
I wish I could always have something to say that

would make everything all right, right now, but I don't. I do know one thing, though:

WHATEVER COMES TO ANY OF US
IS SENT OR ALLOWED BY GOD.

To some people, that may make God sound weak, uncaring, or even sadistic, but when you're facing the real world it helps to remember that God is in control. He is still at work, even when we feel that our suffering will never end. Like the psalmist commanded, we must "hope. . .in God" (Psalm 42:5 KJV).

BARBARA JOHNSON
The Best of Barbara Johnson

Find Your True Self

*"Naked I came from my mother's womb,
and naked I will depart. The LORD gave
and the LORD has taken away; may the
name of the LORD be praised."*

JOB 1:21 NIV

There is no ongoing spiritual life without this process of letting go. At the precise point where we refuse, growth stops. If we hold tightly to anything given to us, unwilling to let it go when the time comes to let it go or unwilling to allow it to be used as the Giver means it to be used, we stunt the growth of the soul.

It is easy to make a mistake here. "If God gave it to me," we say, "it's mine. I can do what I want with it." No. The truth is that it is ours to thank

Him for and ours to offer back to Him, ours to re-linquish, ours to lose, ours to let go of—if we want to find our true selves, if we want real Life, if our hearts are set on glory.

ELISABETH ELLIOT
Passion and Purity

Sweet Deliverance

She said to herself, "If I only touch his cloak,
I will be healed."

MATTHEW 9:21 NIV

O My child, I am coming to thee walking upon
the waters of the sorrows of thy life; yea, above the
sounds of the storm ye shall hear My voice calling
thy name.

Ye are never alone, for I am at thy right hand.
Never despair, for I am watching over and caring
for thee. Be not anxious. What seemeth to thee
to be at present a difficult situation is all part of
My planning, and I am working out the details of
circumstances to the end that I may bless thee and
reveal Myself to thee in a new way.

As I have opened thine eyes to see, so shall
I open thine ears to hear, and ye shall come to
know Me even as did Moses, yea, in a face-to-face
relationship.

For I shall remove the veil that separates Me from thee and ye shall know Me as thy dearest Friend and as thy truest Comforter.

No darkness shall hide the shining of My face, for I shall be to thee as a bright star in the night sky. Never let thy faith waver. Reach out thy hand, and thou shalt touch the hem of My garment.

FRANCES J. ROBERTS
Come Away My Beloved

Light at the End
of the Tunnel

The people who walk in darkness will see a great light.
For those who live in a land of deep darkness,
a light will shine.

ISAIAH 9:2 NLT

Are you in need of a glimmer of light at the end of the tunnel? Isaiah promises that even in darkness, even in death itself, there is good ground for hope. The power of God is able to restore life to His people even when they appear already dead!

What is that great light? It is the Savior, Jesus Christ. This prediction was fulfilled by Christ's coming (Matthew 4:16). The light of Christ brought the promise of deliverance for Israel. A new day had come!

The Savior is a great light in the darkness to us as well. Maybe you live in the darkness of divorce or in the shadow of death. Some of you may be watching a loved one slowly disintegrate before your eyes. Perhaps you have given up seeing any light in a dark family or church situation. Others, in seemingly perfect circumstances, live in the deepest darkness of all—depression that nothing seems to penetrate! Listen to the Good News! There's light at the end of the tunnel—look up and see Jesus standing there! Hear what He says: "I am the light of the world. If you follow me, you won't have to walk in darkness, because you will have the light that leads to life" (John 8:12 NLT).

The Word of God penetrates the darkness of our soul. It's as if God penetrates the darkness with His inescapable light. Ask God to penetrate your tunnel of darkness with His glorious light.

JILL BRISCOE
The One Year Book of Devotions for Women

Unfailing Love

*Every good and perfect gift is from above, coming
down from the Father of the heavenly lights,
who does not change like shifting shadows.*

JAMES 1:17 NIV

God is not moody, loving us one day and raging against us the next. He does not change His good intentions toward us. Daily He extends new mercies and looks for our open hands, into which He wants to deposit invaluable, immeasurable blessings. He is always faithful to deliver on His promises.

We tend to be suspicious of God because we see Him through the haze of what our own hearts are capable of. *We* change our minds. *We* feel stingy or generous on any given day depending on how others treat us. *We* are reserved with others based on past hurts and disappointments.

But His ways are not our ways. His thoughts
are not our thoughts. God keeps short accounts.
He does not superimpose the past over the future.
He is able to let bygones be bygones. So no matter
what you have done, He is ready to start anew. He's
ready to start blessing you all over again.

Don't you just love that about Him?

MICHELLE MCKINNEY HAMMOND
How to Be Blessed and Highly Favored

Making Payments

"If any of you wants to be my follower, you must
turn from your selfish ways, take up your cross daily,
and follow me. If you try to hang on to your life,
you will lose it. But if you give up your life
for my sake, you will save it."

LUKE 9:23–24 NLT

When you buy a house you first make a large down payment. Then, to keep the house, you must make a smaller payment every time it comes due. You can't change your mind and say, "I don't feel like making payments!" without serious consequences.

The same is true of your relationship with God. To make Him your permanent dwelling place, your initial down payment consists of making Him Lord over your life. After that, ongoing payments must be made, which means saying yes whenever God directs you to do something. They are all a part of the purchase, but one happens initially and the other is eternally ongoing (just like house payments!). The difference is that the Lord will take only as much payment from me as I am willing to give Him. And I can possess only as much of what He has for me as I am willing to secure with my obedience.

STORMIE OMARTIAN
Praying God's Will for Your Life

Mighty Sermons

When Jesus saw his ministry drawing huge crowds, he climbed a hillside. Those who were apprenticed to him, the committed, climbed with him. Arriving at a quiet place, he sat down and taught his climbing companions.

MATTHEW 5:1-2 MSG

The unique illustrations given by Dr. Talmage always interested me, one of them in particular. In a Christmas sermon he told the story of a little Swiss girl who was dying; and from her window she could look out to the lofty summit of the mountains amid which she had been reared. "Papa, carry me to the tip of the mountain," she exclaimed. But he replied, "My child, I cannot carry you, but the angels will." For a time she was silent and lay with her eyes closed. At length she opened them and looking out of the window exclaimed in her joy, "They *are* carrying me, father. I shall soon be at the top." With those words Dr. Talmage concluded his sermon. It seemed to his hearers that he had conducted them to a high pinnacle in a lofty range of mountains where they might breath a pure atmosphere. When I reminded him of the beautiful effect that his words had upon us, he said, "Ah, you are right. I never intended to bring you down from that summit."

And thus it is with even the humblest fellow-ministers; they take us to heights of which the soul often dreams, yet rarely attains, in fact to those mansions of the blest where there are always light and warmth and love; where the thirst of weary pilgrims is quenched by draughts of mountain springs; and where this mortal spirit puts on its immortality.

FANNY CROSBY
Memories of Eighty Years

Loving Purpose

"With God all things are possible."

MATTHEW 19:26 NIV

*I*t is almost impossible to estimate the power of purpose in life. Things thought out of reason have been accomplished through purpose. Kingdoms have been torn down and built again, heathen customs have been uprooted and the light of Christianity put in their places, men born under the bondage of hard and unfavorable circumstances have risen above their environments and been powers in the world, the mysteries of the earth and sky have been sought out and their power put to work for mankind, yes, every great and noble deed that has ever been done has had for its captain and soldiers men and women of strong purpose.

I once read of a woman upon a lonely ranch in a foreign land. Her husband had to go away for a week or more, leaving her alone for that time with her little children. He had not been gone long before she was bitten by a poisonous serpent, and she knew that in a few hours, not more than eight, she must die. She remembered her children and that if they were to be kept safe she must in the time left her draw enough water and bake enough bread to supply them until their father returned, or he might find his family all dead. So she worked and prayed that day, sick, fainting, almost unconscious, but love set her purpose strong, and she struggled on. Night came, and her hours were nearly up. She put her babes to bed and wandered out of sight of the cabin to die, but with a determination to live as long as possible for her children's sake. And, morning found her still alive, still walking, and her system beginning to clear from the poison. She lived to tell the story, a monument to the power of a loving purpose.

MABEL HALE
Beautiful Girlhood

Does He Forget Me?

*Why are you downcast, O my soul? Why so
disturbed within me? Put your hope in God,
for I will yet praise him, my Savior and my God.*

PSALM 42:11 NIV

Sometimes I experienced moments of great
despair. I remember one night when I was outside
the barracks on my way to roll call. The stars were
beautiful. I remember saying, "Lord, You guide all
those stars. You have not forgotten them but You
have forgotten Betsie and me."

Then Betsie said, "No, He has not forgotten us.
I know that from the Bible. The Lord Jesus said, 'I
am with you always, until the end of the world,' and
Corrie, He is here with us. We must believe that. It
is not what we are *feeling* that counts, but what we
believe!"

Feelings come and feelings go
And feelings are deceiving.
My warrant is the Word of God,
None else is worth believing.

I slowly learned not to trust in myself or my faith or my feelings, but to trust in Him. Feelings come and go—they are deceitful. In all that hell around us, the promises from the Bible kept us sane.

CORRIE TEN BOOM
Jesus Is Victor

A Test of Faith

The LORD will fulfill his purpose for me;
your love, O LORD, endures forever—
do not abandon the works of your hands.

PSALM 138:8 NIV

At some point in our lives, most of us will face a faith test. It is in that moment in time when what we have always believed about who God is and what He allows to happen in our lives intersects with the reality of our experiences—a head-on collision between our faith and the hard facts of an impossible situation. It's a time when we sometimes question the goodness of God because we are having difficulty understanding what "trust" looks like. On the surface, nothing makes sense. We relive the scene of an accident or we remember the details of watching a loved one die—too early. We mentally revisit the hospital room when the doctor tactfully reports that our newborn baby has a serious birth defect.

Over time, we wrestle with the question, is God trustworthy? The outward appearance for the situation does not indicate that God intervened in our circumstances. Will we cut and run from our relationship with God, or will we rely on Him and believe His character is still good?

CAROL KENT
A New Kind of Normal

Hope in His Promises

It is better to take refuge in the
LORD than to trust in man.

PSALM 118:8 NIV

Do it! Choose Jesus Christ! Deny yourself, take up the Cross, and follow Him—for the world must be shown. The world must see, in us, a discernible, visible, startling difference.

Put your trust in Him. Not in people or circumstances or dreams or programs or plans, not in any human notion of what will or won't happen, but in the God of Abraham, Isaac, and Jacob, of Daniel and all the others—the God whose Son went through the darkest valleys so that you and I might be saved. If somebody was willing to give his life for you, would you trust him? Of course you would. Jesus loved you then. He loves you now. He'll be loving you every minute of every hour of every day of the rest of your life, and no matter what happens, nothing can separate you from that love. I know it's true. I have found that sure and steadfast Refuge in my Lord and Savior—the only real safety—the Everlasting Arms! I've walked with God a long time. I know He keeps His promises.

ELISABETH ELLIOT
Secure in the Everlasting Arms

Soul Food

Jesus answered, "It is written: 'Man does not live on bread alone, but on every word that comes from the mouth of God.'"

MATTHEW 4:4 NIV

At times in my battle with fear and depression I sat down to read the Word of God feeling so depleted, numb, or preoccupied with my mental state that I could hardly even comprehend the words. I not only didn't feel close to God but felt it futile to hope He could ever change me or my life in any lasting way. In spite of that, as I read I was struck by a remarkable lifting of those negative emotions. Afterward I may not have been able to pass a Bible school quiz on the passage, but I felt renewed, strengthened, and hopeful.

When you feel confused, fearful, depressed, or anxious, take the Bible in hand and say, "This book is on my side. My soul is starving, and this is food for my spirit. I want to do the right thing and reading the Bible is always the right thing to do. Lord, I thank You for Your Word. Reveal Yourself to me as I read it and let it come alive in my heart and mind. Show me what I need for my life today. Let Your Word penetrate through anything that would block me from receiving it."

Then begin to read until you sense peace coming into your heart.

STORMIE OMARTIAN
Finding Peace for Your Heart

Hope in His Name

"I am the Alpha and the Omega,"
says the Lord God, "who is, and who was,
and who is to come, the Almighty."

REVELATION 1:8 NIV

In the Gospel of John Christ adopts this name
of "I am" as His own. These simple words, I am,
express eternity and unchangeableness of existence,
which is the very first element necessary in a God
who is to be depended upon. No dependence could
be placed by anyone of us upon a changeable God.
He must be the same yesterday, today, and forever,
if we are to have any peace or comfort.

But is this all His name implies, simply "I am"?
I am what? we ask. What does this "I am" include?
It includes everything the human heart longs for
and needs. This unfinished name of God seems
to me like a blank check signed by a rich friend

given to us to be filled in with whatever sum we may desire. The whole Bible tells us what it means. Every attribute of God, every revelation of His character, every proof of His undying love, every declaration of His watchful care, every assertion of His purposes of tender mercy, every manifestation of His loving kindness—all are the filling out of this unfinished "I am." God tells us through all the pages of His Book what He is. "I am," He says, "I am all that my people need" "I am their Strength"; "I am their Wisdom"; "I am their righteousness"; "I am their peace"; "I am their salvation"; "I am their life"; "I am their all in all!"

This apparently unfinished name, therefore, is the most comforting name the heart of man could devise, because it allows us to add to it, without any limitation, whatever we feel the need of, and even "exceeding abundantly" beyond all that we can ask or think.

HANNAH WHITALL SMITH
The God of All Comfort

He Is All We Need

Whom have I in heaven but you?
And earth has nothing I desire besides you.

*G*rowing is not always easy, but it is the only way to blossom.

I find many people today who are looking for things that offer a certain measure of self-esteem and self-confidence in a variety of places—a job, spouse, higher education, etc. And while these things are good, they only offer limited satisfaction. Others seek self-esteem or fulfillment in the wrong places. They look for love, but they look for it in an affair. They seek security but seek it in a mate, job, or stock portfolio. They long for a sense of peace and serenity but seek it in a bottle of alcohol or pills. They desire self-esteem, so they acquire possessions and status symbols. One of the greatest examples Mother has been to me is of a woman who has not looked to anything or anyone to be to her what only Jesus Christ can be.

You see, all we need and desire, HE IS. At some point in each of our lives, God will bring us to a place where He will prove this to us.

GIGI GRAHAM TCHIVIDJIAN
A Quiet Knowing

The Power of Prayer

I will give you thanks, for you answered me;
you have become my salvation.

PSALM 118:21 NIV

$\mathscr{I}$ heard about a terrible criminal who had just been condemned to death for some horrible crimes. Everything would lead one to believe that he would die without repenting. I wanted at all cost to prevent him from going to hell. In order to do that I used every imaginable means: Sensing that in myself I could do nothing, I offered to God all the infinite merits of Our Lord and the treasures of the Holy Church. Finally I begged [my aunt] to have a Mass said for my intentions. Deep in my heart I felt certainty that my desires would be granted, but in order to give myself courage to continue to pray for sinners, I told God that I was quite sure that He would forgive the poor miserable criminal, and that I would believe this even if he did not confess and showed no sign of repentance, so much did I have confidence in Jesus' infinite mercy, but I asked Him only for "a sign" of repentance simply for my consolation. . . .

My prayer was granted to the letter! I put my hand on the newspaper *La Croix*. I opened it hurriedly, and what did I see? . . . Oh! My tears betrayed my emotion, and I was obliged to go hide. . . . The criminal had not confessed; he had climbed up onto the scaffold and was getting ready to put his head into the ominous opening in the guillotine, when suddenly, gripped with a sudden inspiration, he turned back, grabbed a Crucifix that the priest was holding up to him, and kissed its sacred wounds three times! Then his soul went to receive the merciful judgment of the One who declares that in heaven there will be more joy for a single sinner who repents than for ninety-nine righteous persons who have no need for repentance! (Luke 15:7).

SAINT THERESE OF LISIEUX
The Story of a Soul

Depend on Him

"Ask and it will be given to you; seek and you will find; knock and the door will be opened to you."

MATTHEW 7:7 NIV

O My children, what do you need today? Is it comfort; is it courage; is it healing; is it guidance? Lo, I say unto thee, that whatever it is that ye need, if ye will look to Me, I will supply.

I will be to thee what the sun is to the flower; what the water of the ocean is to the fish; and what the sky is to the birds. For I will be the giver to thee of life and light and strength. I will surround thee and preserve thee, so that in Me ye may live, move, and have your being, existing in Me when apart from Me ye would die. Yea, I will be to thee as the wide open skies, in that I will liberate thy spirit in such fashion that ye shall not be earthbound.

Ye shall live in a realm where the things of earth shall not be able to impede and obstruct and limit thy movement; but ye shall be freed in Me to a place where thy spirit may soar as the eagle, and ye may make your nest in a place of safety and solitude, unmolested and undefiled by the sordidness of the world.

Thou shalt have companionship; but it shall be the companionship of those like-minded with thee, yea, of those who like thyself have been done with the beggarly elements, and whose sense of value has been readjusted so that they deem the unseen as of greater value than the seen, and the spiritual riches more precious than the wealth of the world.

Be done with petty things. Be done with small dreams. Give Me all that you have and are; and I will share with you abundantly all that I have and all that I am.

FRANCES J. ROBERTS
Come Away My Beloved

Jehovah-Tsidkenu

"For the time is coming," says the LORD, "when I will raise up a righteous descendant from King David's line. He will be a King who rules with wisdom. He will do what is just and right throughout the land. And this will be his name: 'The LORD Is Our Righteousness.' In that day Judah will be saved, and Israel will live in safety."

JEREMIAH 23:5–6 NLT

Many of us look back to the good old days. But Israel was told by Jeremiah to look forward to the good new days that lay ahead. Jehovah Himself would provide not only a lamb for an atoning sacrifice, but a hope for the future. Psychologists tell us people cannot function without hope. Yet many people today feel a hopelessness that never seems to go away.

Without Christ there is no hope for the future because He is the future. God holds the future as surely as He holds the past and the present. He is working His purposes out. He knows the plans that

184

He has for us: plans of good and not of disaster. Without God, without Christ, without hope, we are lost people groping in the dark for some meaning to life.

"The time is coming," says the Lord, when He will provide one who will put all things in their proper place. Rights will be respected and wrongs redressed. There will be salvation and security for God's people. This is our hope. There's a new day coming for the believer.

Jehovah-Tsidkenu gives us that new day, that hope, that future. Do you feel hopeless? "Hope in God" (Psalm 42:5 NLT).

JILL BRISCOE
The One Year Book of Devotions for Women

His Good Work in You

And I am certain that God, who began the good work within you, will continue his work until it is finally finished on the day when Christ Jesus returns.

PHILIPPIANS 1:6 NLT

Do you have an impossible job to do? Has the Lord told you to do it? Go ahead! When we pray, we enter God's domain from the domain of our inability. He is conqueror and makes us more than conquerors. It is not bad if we feel weak, if our inability is a reality to us. That's exactly when the Lord does miracles. Paul said, "When I am weak, then I am strong." Do you know why I thought it so important that these people in that country learned to forgive? Jesus said that if we do not forgive, we will not be forgiven, and we break down the bridge that we need for ourselves. Jesus is coming again very soon, and we must be prepared—by being in good relationship with God and with others. We can't get it together ourselves, however hard we try. But if we place our weak hand in the strong hand of Jesus, then He does it. Jesus is looking forward to His return to earth and it is He who is preparing us for His return. Surrender to Him completely. He who began a good work in you will bring it to completion on that day—the day of His second coming.

Corrie ten Boom
Reflections of God's Glory

Title Index

Contributors

Michelle Medlock Adams has a diverse résumé featuring inspirational books, children's picture books, and greeting cards. Her insights have appeared in periodicals across America, including *Today's Christian Woman* and *Guideposts for Kids*. She lives in Fort Worth, Texas, with her husband, two daughters, and a "mini petting zoo."

Corrie ten Boom was simply an ordinary, middle-aged Dutch spinster when the Second World War began. By the time the conflict ended, she was literally transformed by the faith she had merely accepted, and on a mission from God. By God's grace, Corrie survived the concentration camp and became a "tramp for the Lord," sharing in more than sixty nations the thrilling message that nothing, not even death, can separate us from God's love.

Jill Briscoe is the author of more than forty books—including devotionals, study guides, poetry, and children's books. She serves as executive editor of *Just Between Us* magazine and served on the board of World Relief and *Christianity Today* for more than twenty years. Jill and her husband make their home in Milwuakee, Wisconsin.

Amy Carmichael (1867–1951) was a Protestant Christian missionary in India, who opened an orphanage and founded a mission in Dohnavur. She served in India for fifty-six years without furlough and authored many books about her missionary work.

Fanny Crosby (1820–1915), blinded at infancy, became one of the most popular and prolific of all hymn writers. She wrote more than eight thousand hymns in her lifetime, including the best-known "Blessed Assurance," "Jesus Is Tenderly Calling You Home," "Praise Him, Praise Him," and "To God Be the Glory."

Elisabeth Elliot is a best-selling author of more than twenty books including *Passion and Purity*, *Be Still My Soul*, *The Path of Loneliness*, and *Keep a Quiet Heart*. She and her husband, Lars Gren, make their home in Magnolia, Massachusetts.

Carol L. Fitzpatrick is a best-selling author of nine books that have totaled nearly three quarters of a million books sold. She is a frequent conference speaker for writing groups and church groups. Carol and her husband have three grown children and three grandchildren. Although she credits her Midwest upbringing for instilling her core values, she has lived in California for nearly four decades.

Mabel Hale lived in Wichita, Kansas, in the early twentieth century. *Beautiful Girlhood* was her most popular book.

Michelle McKinney Hammond is a best-selling author, speaker, singer, and television cohost. She has authored more than thirty books including best-selling titles *The Diva Principle*; *Sassy, Single, and Satisfied*; *101 Ways to Get and Keep His Attention*; and *Secrets of an Irresistible Woman*. She makes her home in Chicago.

Jocelyn Hamsher is a gifted Bible study teacher, writer, board member and speaker for Circle of Friends Ministries. She lives in Sugarcreek, Ohio, with her husband, Bruce, and their three sons. She enjoys spending time with family, studying the Word of God, drinking coffee, and laughing with her husband.

Lisa Harper is an excellent communicator, author, speaker, and Bible teacher. She has spoken at Women of Faith, Moody Bible, Winsome Women, and Focus on the Family conferences and has written a number of books including *A Perfect Mess: How God Adores and Transforms Imperfect People Like Us.*

Frances Ridley Havergal (1836–1879) was an English poet and hymn writer. "Take My Life and Let It Be" is one of her best-known hymns. She also wrote hymn melodies, religious tracts, and works for children.

Missy Horsfall is a published magazine and greeting card writer and coauthor of the novel *Love Me Back to Life.* A pastor's wife, she is a speaker and Bible study teacher for Circle of Friends and serves on the board overseeing their writing ministries. Missy also produces and cohosts the COF radio program.

Sharon Jaynes is the author of thirteen books with Harvest House Publishers, Focus on the Family, and Moody Publishers and a frequent guest on national radio and television. She has also written numerous magazine articles and devotions for publications such as *Focus on the Family, Decision, Crosswalk.com,* and *In Touch.*

Barbara Johnson (1927–2007), was an award-winning author and Women of Faith Speaker Emeritus with more than four million books in print and translated into ten foreign languages. She faced her long battle with cancer with the same humor and wisdom she met the many adversities of her life.

Carol Kent is an internationally known speaker and author. Her books include *When I Lay My Isaac Down, Becoming a Woman of Influence,* and *Mothers Have Angel Wings.* She is president of Speak Up Speaker Services and the founder and director of Speak Up With Confidence seminars.

Virelle Kidder is a full-time writer and conference speaker and author of six books including *Meet Me at the Well* and *The Best Life Ain't Easy.* She is published in national magazines such as *Moody Magazine, Focus on the Family's Pastor's Family, Decision, Pray!, Journey, HomeLife,* and *Tapestry.*

Donna K. Maltese is a freelance writer, editor, and proofreader; publicist for a local Mennonite project; and the assistant director of RevWriter Writers Conferences. Donna resides in Bucks County, Pennsylvania, with her husband and two children. She is a pastor's prayer partner and is active in her local church.

Gena Maselli is a Texan and full-time writer who has spent over a decade developing materials for worldwide Christian ministries. She now writes devotionals, nonfiction, and magazine and Internet articles.

Pamela L. McQuade is a freelance writer and editor in Nutley, New Jersey, who has worked with numerous publishers. Her Barbour credits include *The Word on Life*, *Daily Wisdom for Couples*, and *Prayers and Promises*, all coauthored with Toni Sortor. Pam and her husband share their home with basset hounds and are involved in basset hound rescue.

Janine Miller grew up in Holmes County, Ohio. She currently homeschools her children, ages five to fifteen, and works part-time from her home as a church secretary. Janine and her husband of twenty-three years live in southern Ohio with their four children.

Stormie Omartian is a popular writer, speaker, and author. She is author of the bestselling The Power of Praying® books as well as many other titles. She and her husband have been married thirty years and have three grown children.

Donna Partow is an author and motivational speaker. Her books, including *This Isn't The Life I Signed Up For. . .But I'm Finding Hope and Healing* and *Becoming a Vessel God Can Use*, have sold almost a million copies and her ministry, Pieces4Peace, reaches into the largest Muslim city in the world.

Becki Reiser is wife to Jeff and mother to three grown boys and one daughter. After the murder of their seventeen-year-old daughter, Jeff and Becki began a ministry of sharing their testimony of forgiveness. Becki is a contributing author in Standard Publishing's *Devotions* magazine and Circle of Friends website, www.circleoffriends.fm.

Ramona Richards is a freelance writer and editor living in Tennessee. Formerly the editor of *Ideals* magazine, Ramona has also edited children's books, fiction, nonfiction, study Bibles, and reference books for major Christian publishers. She is the author of *A Moment with God for Single Parents*.

Bobbie Rill is a motivational speaker and life coach. As a Licensed Professional Counselor, she served as executive director over a multi-state network of Christian counseling and educational centers. She also directed Women of Virtue, a national conference and radio ministry. She and her husband, Bob, reside in Tucson, Arizona.

Frances J. Roberts (1918–2009) is best known for her classic devotional *Come Away My Beloved*. She founded The King's Press in 1964, where she authored and published *Come Away* and eight other books, selling over 1.5 million copies in the last thirty years.

Emily Smith lives in Greenfield, Indiana, with her wonderful husband, Eric. Married for two years, the only children they currently have are four-legged. Emily works for a home health agency and is a weekly blogger for the Circle of Friends website. She loves reading, cooking, and spending time with family.

Hannah Whitall Smith (1832–1911) was born into a strict Quaker home in Philadelphia and became a major influence in the Holiness movement of the late nineteenth century. Besides *The Christian's Secret of a Happy Life*, Smith also wrote *The God of All Comfort* and an autobiography, *The Unselfishness of God and How I Discovered It*.

Joyce Strong is an author and international conference speaker whose books include *Journey to Joy; Leading with Passion and Grace; Instruments for His Glory; Lambs on the Ledge; Caught in the Crossfire; Of Dreams and Kings and Mystical Things; A Dragon, A Dreamer;* and *The Promise Giver*.

Gigi Graham Tchividjian, daughter of Billy and Ruth Graham, is a busy wife, mother, grandmother, author, and speaker. She currently writes a regular column for *Christian Parenting* magazine and has written four books, including *Weather of the Heart* and *A Search for Serenity*.

Saint Therese of Lisieux (1873–1897) became a French Carmelite nun at the age of fifteen. Her memoir, *Story of a Soul*, inspired thousands to recognize God's unique call on their lives. She was canonized by Pope Pius XI in 1925.

Sheila Walsh is a unique combination of international author, speaker, worship leader, television talk show host, and Bible teacher. She is a speaker with Women of Faith and best-selling author of her memoir *Honestly* and the Gold Medallion Award nominee *The Heartache No One Sees*.

Permissions

Will for Your Life, Stormie Omartian, Copyright ©
2001, Thomas Nelson Inc., Nashville, Tennessee.)
All rights reserved.

"Hope in Purpose" taken from *The Power of a
Praying Woman* (Copyright © 2002 by Stormie
Omartian); published by Harvest House
Publishers, Eugene, OR 97402.
www.harvesthousepublishers.com. Used by
permission.

"Hope in the Truth" by Virelle Kidder. Used by
permission.

"Your Song Is Coming" taken from *Meet Me at the
Well* by Virelle Kidder. Copyright © 2008. "Your
Song Is Coming" taken from *The Best Life Ain't
Easy, But It's Worth It* by Virelle Kidder. Copyright
© 2008, Moody Publishers. Used by Permission.

Scripture Index

OLD TESTAMENT

WHAT IS CIRCLE OF FRIENDS?

Circle of Friends Ministries, Inc. is a nonprofit
organization established to build a pathway for
women to come into a personal relationship with
Jesus Christ and to build Christian unity among
women. Our mission is to honor Jesus Christ
through meeting the needs of women in our local,
national, and international communities. Our
vision is to be women who are committed to Jesus
Christ, obediently seeking God's will and fulfilling
our life mission as Christ-followers. As individuals and as a corporate group, we minister Christ-
centered hope, biblically based encouragement,
and unconditional love by offering God-honoring,
Word-based teaching, worship, accountability, and
fellowship to women in a nondenominational envi-
ronment through speaker services, worship teams,
daily web blogs and devotionals, radio programs,
and GirlFriends teen events.

COF also partners with churches and women's
groups to bring conferences, retreats, Bible studies,

concerts, simulcasts, and servant evangelism projects to their communities. We have a Marketplace Ministry teaching kingdom principles in the workplace and are committed to undergird, with prayer and financial support, foreign mission projects that impact the world for Jesus Christ. Our goal is to evangelize the lost and edify the body of Christ, by touching the lives of women—locally, nationally, and globally.